MEMORY MAKERS

Family Tree page ideas
for Scrapbookers

130 ways to create a scrapbook legacy

Executive Editor *Kerry Arquette*

Founder *Michele Gerbrandt*

Senior Editor *MaryJo Regier*

Art Director *Andrea Zocchi*

Designer *Nick Nyffeler*

Production Designer *Robin Rozum*

Art Acquisitions Editor *Janetta Abucejo Wieneke*

Craft Editor *Jodi Amidei*

Photographer *Ken Trujillo*

Contributing Photographers *Brenda Martinez, Ruth Ann Praska, Jennifer Reeves*

Contributing Writers *Kelly Angard, MaryJo Regier, Allison Stacy, Maureen Taylor*

Editorial Support *Karen Cain, Emily Curry Hitchingham, Lydia Rueger, Dena Twinem*

Memory Makers® Family Tree Page Ideas for Scrapbookers
Copyright © 2004 Memory Makers Books
All rights reserved.

Published by Memory Makers Books, an imprint of F+W Publications, Inc.
12365 Huron Street, Suite 500, Denver, CO 80234
Phone 1-800-254-9124
First edition. Printed in the United States.
08 07 06 05 5 4 3 2

Library of Congress Cataloging-in-Publication Data

Family tree page ideas for scrapbookers : 125 ways to create a scrapbook legacy.-- 1st ed.
    p. cm.
  ISBN 1-892127-42-3
    1. Photograph albums. 2. Photographs--Conversation and restoration. 3. Scrapbooks. 4.
Genealogy. I. Memory Makers Books.

TR465.F36 2004
745.593--dc22

                                                                    2004053649

Distributed to trade and art markets by
F+W Publications, Inc.
4700 East Galbraith Road, Cincinnati, OH 45236
Phone 1-800-289-0963

ISBN 1-892127-42-3

Memory Makers Books is the home of *Memory Makers*, the scrapbook magazine dedicated to educating and inspiring scrapbookers. To subscribe, or for more information, call 1-800-366-6465.
Visit us on the Internet at www.memorymakersmagazine.com

THIS BOOK BELONGS TO

We dedicate this book to all of our Memory Makers' contributors who shared their amazing family tree scrapbook pages with us and to scrapbookers everywhere who may be inspired to trace their ancestry so that future descendants may experience the connecting bond of heritage.

Table of Contents

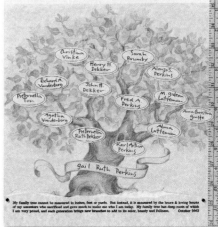

Traditional Trees 14-39

Select from a wide array of fresh and innovative approaches for documenting family relationships in a customary, tree-shape format using preprinted tree papers or creating your own clever, handmade trees. Discover how to make trees from paper, tree photos, organic materials, metallics, fabric, fibers and various colorants. Play with quilling, painting, stenciling, stitching, punching and embossing techniques to grow an eye-pleasing remembrance of your ancestry.

Pedigree Charts 40-63

A filled pedigree chart is one of the crowning glories of genealogical research—whether generated on the computer, downloaded from the Internet or handmade. Learn how to present your historic family information in a format that is easy to understand. These ideas run the gamut from simple to elaborate, structured to freestyle, historical to contemporary, as well as colorful charts that make a handsome statement in your scrapbook or to display on the wall.

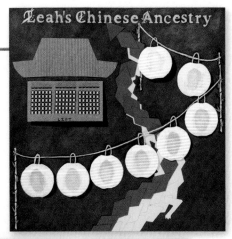

Cultivating Culture 64-77

Celebrate your ethnic heritage in traditional style with scrapbook page elements based on designs and patterns from the culture of your ancestors. Uncover smart ways to infuse authenticity on your pages with maps, flags, folk art, patterns, clip art, history, heraldry and country symbols and icons. Immerse yourself in the traditions and customs of your ancestral homeland for pages that speak not only to the heart but that cultivate true ethnic pride.

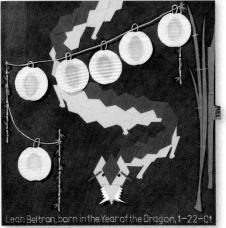

Growing a Hybrid 78-107

Check out these fun ideas for documenting those distinctive family traits that stand out as something truly unique. From heirloom dresses and beloved ships to patronymic naming patterns and generations of wild hairstyles, it's all here! Find numerous interesting ways to preserve those comical family tidbits and refreshingly interesting morsels that really make your family history anything but commonplace. Nothing's off limits with hybrids; after all, it's all relative.

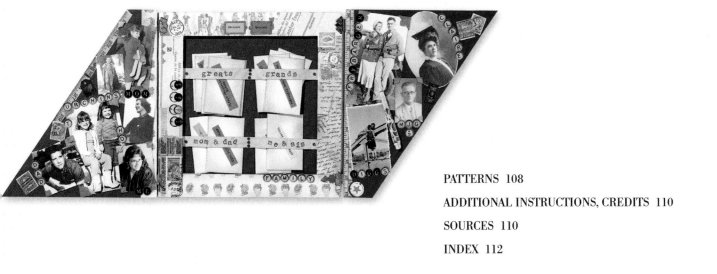

Introduction

Researching your family heritage is one of scrapbooking's most rewarding experiences. It is a curious blend of sleuthing and surprises, dedication and discovery, perseverance and personal growth, but most of all—connection!

I first embarked on an ancestral journey when I discovered there was software to help me organize the information. The user-friendly databases made me realize that even I could do this. The software helped me determine how best to include stepfamily in my tree. This research gave me the opportunity to get in touch with relatives and say, "Hi! So what is your middle name and when were you born?" I realized how little I knew about my living relatives, let alone past ancestors. I struck a gem when I found a great-uncle who had researched one side of our family all the way back to a village in Sicily. We have collaborated ever since. Once I had all of the information organized, I created family trees for my children's bloodlines and sent members books for Christmas. Though I realize they may not appreciate it today, I know someday they will.

I do know that creating family trees for scrapbooks takes time. The research and gathering of photos and data can seem overwhelming. And brainstorming a concise way to convey the information on a scrapbook page for future generations can be a daunting task. Whether you are an amateur genealogist who is new to scrapbooking or a seasoned scrapbook veteran new to genealogy, this book is just for you! Memory Makers *Family Tree Page Ideas for Scrapbookers* strikes at the root of family tree fear, branching out with ease into a rich display of scrapbook art.

We launch the book with expert genealogical research and product tips for beginners and include ideas for growing an ancestral photo collection and taming the paper tiger that is likely to spring up during your research. The pinnacle of this book is the most innovative family tree page ideas ever presented in one complete, user-friendly source. Some of our favorite pages submitted as part of a recent Memory Makers Family Tree Contest, and others sent in by talented readers, are included.

Inside, you'll find a wide variety of hand-crafted family trees, pedigree chart ideas and creative techniques to make the process fun and accomplishable! Featured are unique, one-of-a-kind family trees with ideas for every creative style—from elegant to whimsical and cutting-edge contemporary to culturally inspired. So begin today on a journey into the yesteryear of your ancestors and discover how your labor of love can sprout into a historical piece of art that will be cherished for generations!

Michele

Michele Gerbrandt
Founding Editor
Memory Makers magazine

Getting Started

It starts innocently enough. Maybe you want to discover the story behind a mysterious family photo. Perhaps you're curious where you got your sideways smile or you want to leave a legacy for your children. So you poke around in family papers. Type relatives' names into Internet databases. Chat with Great-Aunt Bertha. And the discoveries amaze you. It's easy to get hooked on uncovering your family's past. Just think how exciting it would be to find a photo of Great-Grandma's mercantile, or Grandpa's enlistment papers—and what wonderful material that would make for your scrapbooks. Here you'll find tools to help you begin tracing your roots so you can make the amazing discoveries that will inspire you to create your own family tree scrapbook pages.

Beginners' Research Tips

Just as every stellar scrapbook page starts with basic elements—background paper, pictures, journaling—all family history research follows a familiar process. Let's walk through guidelines for getting started.

LEARN TO NAVIGATE YOUR FAMILY TREE Study basic genealogical terms and familiarize yourself with family history forms. In genealogy-ese, the basic family tree form is called a pedigree chart—you'll record your ancestors on that. Use a family group sheet to track each nuclear family member.

RECORD WHAT YOU KNOW On a pedigree chart, write down the family tree details you already have. Keep charts and documents in a research binder to stay organized.

GATHER CLUES FROM AROUND THE HOUSE AND FROM YOUR RELATIVES Look for any documents that might reveal details about your ancestry such as birth certificates, family Bibles, letters, diaries, the back of old photos, obituaries and estate papers. Record new discoveries on your charts.

INTERVIEW OLDER RELATIVES They may know the stories behind the documents you've collected, as well as other family facts. Asking at the outset will save you time trying to find those details on your own.

PICK A FAMILY BRANCH TO RESEARCH It's hard to keep names, dates and family relationships straight, so focus on one ancestor or family line at a time.

FORGET THE RULES OF SPELLING People weren't as finicky about spelling in the past; consequently, you'll find your ancestors' names spelled different ways. Try variations—Stacy, Stacey and Stace, for example—whenever you search an index or database.

WORK BACKWARD AND DON'T SKIP GENERATIONS You might end up tracing the wrong people. Be sure you have the right ancestor, not someone with the same name.

FIND DISTANT COUSINS Someone might have already researched your family tree or possess one-of-a-kind documents that will help you in your research. So post "queries" on Internet message boards and mailing lists.

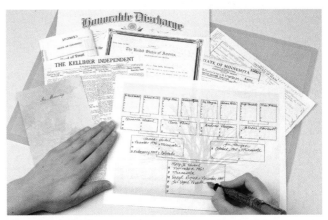

Forget Me Nots offers an array of printable forms to help you corral and organize your genealogical research in various tree and pedigree formats.

FOCUS ON PLACES, NOT JUST PEOPLE Your family's records were created by the jurisdictions where they lived. In the United States, counties, not cities, generally keep records of their residents. And most libraries and archives organize their record collections geographically.

RESEARCH IN RECORDS You'll find records on the Internet, at libraries and in archives. Primary sources (created at the time of an event, such as birth certificates) are more reliable than secondary sources (created after an event, such as online databases). Look for original records and corroborate your findings. Even original records can contain mistakes. Some primary sources include vital records—birth, marriage, divorce and death certificates; federal censuses for every decade from 1790 to 1930; city directories and county histories; deeds and land patents; church and cemetery records; immigration records, including naturalization papers and ship manifests; and the Social Security Death Index (SSDI). Secondary sources can include books and journal articles compiled by other genealogists and newspapers and obituaries.

THINK LIKE A DETECTIVE Check every source, ask other researchers for backup, and don't give up. With patience, determination and creative problem-solving, you can unravel the mystery of your past.

Best-Ever Resources & Tools for Amateur Genealogists

Which tools will help you extend your family tree? Branch out in your research with this roundup of essential family history sources, Web sites, research institutions, beginner publications and genealogy software.

WEB SITES

American Family Immigration History Center at Ellis Island Search digitized passenger lists for the 22 million people who passed through the Port of New York between 1892 and 1924. *www.ellisisland.org*

Ancestry.com The most popular paid genealogy Web site sells access to indexes, transcribed records and digitized original records (including the entire U.S. census). It hosts free message boards and a database of user-contributed family trees. *www.ancestry.com*

Cyndi's List This exhaustive genealogy Web-site directory is the Yahoo! of family history, with more than 200,000 categorized links. *www.cyndislist.com*

FamilySearch The Church of Jesus Christ of Latter-day Saints' genealogy Web site contains searchable databases (transcribed records, the SSDI and user-contributed family files), plus helpful research guides. You also can search the catalog of the Family History Library, the world's largest genealogy library. *www.familysearch.org*

Gencircles This site's free goodies include message boards and a database of user-submitted family tree files. *www.gencircles.com*

Genealogy.com The second biggest subscription genealogy site sells collections of digitized family history books, the U.S. census, immigrant records and user-submitted family trees; it also hosts the free GenForum message boards. *www.genealogy.com*

RootsWeb At RootsWeb, volunteers transcribe records and upload family trees to provide all genealogists with free access to information. The network hosts databases (including the SSDI), mailing lists, message boards and links. *www.rootsweb.com*

US GenWeb Log on here to find free Web sites for genealogical research in every U.S. state and county. *www.usgenweb.org*

LIBRARIES, ARCHIVES & RECORD REPOSITORIES

In addition to public libraries, county courthouses, and state archives and historical societies, these institutions have the best, widest-ranging collections of genealogy materials:

Allen County Public Library 900 Webster St., Fort Wayne, IN 46802, (260) 421-1200. The Allen County library has the world's biggest collection of family history periodicals. *www.acpl.lib.in.us/genealogy*

Family History Library 35 N. West Temple St., Salt Lake City, UT 84150, (801) 240-2331. The Church of Jesus Christ of Latter-day Saints has microfilmed genealogical records from courthouses, archives, cemeteries and churches around the world, and makes them publicly available—for free—here, and at its 3,700-plus branch Family History Centers. Check the Web site to find a center near you. *www.familysearch.org*

National Archives and Records Administration 700 Pennsylvania Ave. NW, Washington, DC 20408, (866) 325-7208. The nation's storehouse for historical records keeps censuses, military records, passenger lists, naturalizations and more. It also has 14 regional research centers. *www.archives.gov*

New England Historic Genealogical Society 101 Newberry St., Boston, MA 02116, (617) 536-5740. A super resource for tracing New England families. *www.newenglandancestors.org*

PUBLICATIONS

The Family Tree Guide Book by the editors of *Family Tree Magazine* (Betterway Books, $19.99)

Family Tree Magazine A bimonthly, beginner-friendly magazine with how-to articles on discovering, preserving and celebrating family history. *www.familytreemagazine.com*

Finding Your Roots Online by Nancy Hendrickson (Betterway Books, $19.99)

Genealogy 101: How to Trace Your Family's History and Heritage by Barbara Renick (Rutledge Hill Press, $19.99)

The Handybook for Genealogists, 10th edition (Everton Publishers, $59.95)

Unpuzzling Your Past, 4th edition, by Emily Anne Croom. A bestselling how-to genealogy guide. (Betterway Books, $18.99).

Your Guide to the Family History Library by Paula Stuart Warren and James W. Warren (Betterway Books, $19.99)

GENEALOGY SOFTWARE

Ancestral Quest 11 Incline Software, (800) 825-8864. (Windows download, $34.95; $39.95 CD-ROM) *www.ancquest.com*

Ancestry Family Tree (800) 262-3787. (Windows, free download) *MyFamily.com; aft.ancestry.com*

Family Trees Quick & Easy 5.0 Individual Software, (800) 822-3522. (Windows, $19.95) *www.individualsoftware.com*

Family Tree Legends Pearl Street Software. (Windows, $49.99) *www.familytreelegends.com*

Family Tree Maker 11 Genealogy.com, (800) 548-1806. (Windows, $29.99) *www.familytreemaker.com*

GEDitCOM 3.11 RSAC Software. (Macintosh, $49.99 shareware) *www.geditcom.com*

Heritage Family Tree Deluxe Individual Software, (800) 822-3522. (Windows, $39.95) *www.individualsoftware.com*

Legacy Family Tree 5.0 Millennia Corp., (800) 753-3453. (Windows, free Standard Edition; $19.95 download or $29.95 CD Deluxe Edition) *www.legacyfamilytree.com*

The Master Genealogist Wholly Genes, (877) 864-3264. (Windows, $39.95 Silver Edition; $79 Gold Edition) *www.whollygenes.com*

Personal Ancestral File 5.2 FamilySearch, (800) 537-5950 (Windows, free download or $6 CD) *www.familysearch.org*

Reunion 8.0 Leister Productions, (717) 697-1378. (Macintosh, $99.95) *www.leisterpro.com*

RootsMagic FormalSoft, (866) 467-6687. Windows, $34.95; $44.95 with printed manual) *www.rootsmagic.com*

Foreign Research Made Simple

Most likely, your genealogical quest eventually will take an international twist: You'll discover an immigrant ancestor. Luckily, you don't need a boat or airplane to follow your family's trail back to the old country—thanks to microfilm and the Web, you can explore your foreign relations right here in America. The key to successful foreign research is to immerse yourself in the country's language, history and record-keeping practices, among other things. Here are a few tips:

KNOW YOUR IMMIGRANT ANCESTOR'S ORIGINAL NAME

Many ancestors adopted new monikers after arriving in America. (Contrary to popular belief, Ellis Island officials didn't change immigrants' names—that's a myth.) In foreign records, ancestors are listed by their original identities, so you'll search for those. Look for native names in family documents and ask older relatives.

PINPOINT YOUR ANCESTRAL TOWN

Once you know whom to look for, you need to know where to find them—and "Italy" or "Mexico" isn't enough. Finding your family's town of origin is crucial. Quiz relatives and check naturalization records, obituaries, family Bibles and other records. Because churches kept local records for centuries, you'll also need to know your family's parish. For that, turn to a gazetteer, or geographical dictionary (available in print, on microfilm and online).

LEARN THE LANGUAGE

Unless your ancestors came from the British Isles, you'll need a translation dictionary to read their records. Get a genealogical one (if available) and learn key terms such as born, from, mother and father. Try online translators, such as *www.babelfish.altavista.com*, but be forewarned: Online translators aren't always 100 percent accurate, and the translation may leave you more confused than the original text you were trying to decipher.

UNDERSTAND THE COUNTRY'S HISTORY

Learn what events led up to your ancestors' departure; you'll likely discover why they emigrated. Study the political history, too, in case a border change put your family's village in a different country. Religious history research can be beneficial when trying to identify and obtain marriage, birth and christening records. Perhaps you're certain your ancestors were all Catholic, but don't be too surprised if you find ancestors of a different faith based on political and social reforms.

GET A GUIDEBOOK

We could write volumes on each country's genealogical peculiarities—in fact, it's already been done. Learn the nitty-gritty from a targeted tome; you'll find titles in the Ethnic Toolkits at *www.familytreemagazine.com*.

SUBSCRIBE TO RELATED MAILING LISTS

Many of the Web sites listed on page 8 have mailing lists related to specific surnames and placenames. By subscribing to specific mailing lists, you join a group of people who are researching the same surname and/or placenames, and all benefit from the exchange of information that takes place through e-mail and the lists' archives. Another benefit: It's a great way to locate and communicate with distant cousins who may be far ahead of you in research and more than willing to share information!

Growing an Ancestral Photo Collection

Telling your family history on a heritage page or in an album requires pictures—either those you own or ones you find. Relatives, Web sites, and antique marts can help you turn a few photos into a hundred if you know where to look and how. Keep in mind that photography dates from 1839 so you won't be able to find photographs of people who died before that date.

IDENTIFY MISSING PIECES

Set a goal to locate pictures of everyone on your family tree (after 1839) and focus on the task one person at a time. Start with your own picture collection in shoe boxes and albums. Double check any genealogical materials such as work badges, licenses and some immigration documents which may include images.

Make a list of family members for whom you lack pictures. Group individuals by nuclear family and carry the inventory, along with copies of any unidentified images with you wherever you go in case you uncover new clues. Follow your progress by highlighting names on your family tree.

REACH OUT TO RELATIVES

The best sources of family photos are relatives who usually have their own collections of images. Begin by contacting all the relatives you know including distant cousins.

Bring along a digital camera on home visits to photograph their images at a high resolution for printing purposes. If someone is willing to send you pictures, ask for good quality, clear photographic or digital copies. A blurry image of a great-grandfather isn't going to work in your page layout.

Ask relatives if they can identify anyone in your pile of unidentified images and don't forget to inquire about family history in general. It might add a new generation or a cache of documents.

FOLLOW YOUR RESEARCH

As you learn more about your ancestors, you'll discover facts that can lead to new photos such as organizational memberships or awards received. Use libraries and archives to search for images in published sources such as trade magazines, newspapers and local biographical encyclopedias.

SPREAD THE WORD

Connect with cousins via online genealogical message boards like those on *www.rootsweb.com*. Communicate your question clearly. Include names and life dates for those of whom you desire to locate pictures, the image formats you'll accept and a brief note about why you need them. Don't include your mailing address or phone number in a publicly posted query; reserve that for a private message.

ONLINE POSSIBILITIES

A few mouse clicks might help you discover new pictures to add to your family archive. Reunion sites reunite people with lost pictures found in antique shops or estate sales. Use *www.cyndislist.com* under "Photographs" to locate some of the more popular sites.

Some sites charge a fee for the images they list. Search for Web sites posted by distant family by typing relevant surnames into a search engine using the image filters to narrow the number of hits or on large Web sites like *www.myfamily.com*.

Follow online auction sites such as *www.Ebay.com* by periodically searching the site or set up an account to be notified when materials, such as items related to your surname and ancestral birthplaces, become available for purchase.

Libraries continue to digitize their picture collections at a rapid rate with many now available on the Web. Check the Web site of the local or state historical society and the public library in the areas in which your ancestors lived. One of the largest online digital picture libraries is the American Memory Project of the Library of Congress, *www.loc.gov*.

TAKE NEW IMAGES

Not having any luck adding old photographs to your family collection? Then expand it by snapping pictures of the events in your everyday life or special occasions so your descendants won't have to look for lost images in the future.

In the end, you probably won't discover photographs of everyone on your list, but you'll have located at least a few new portraits to position on your family layouts. Store all your images in acid- and lignin-free folders and boxes so that these perfect picture solutions for your heritage pages will last.

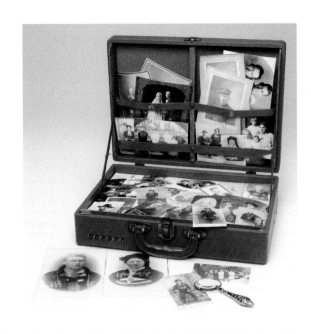

Taming the Paper Tiger

Here are a few tips to manage the documents, letters, pictures and memorabilia you'll acquire in your research. These items accumulate quickly so don't put off implementing these strategies until you're buried in paper. Whether you have one document or a suitcase full of documents, don't locate any new information until you've organized what's on hand. There is no right way to organize. Remember to stick to the basics and file regularly so you'll be able to find a document when you need it.

Generations' Photo and Memory Express storage totes have plenty of room and dividers for organizing photos and documents for different surnames until you are ready to scrapbook.

SET REALISTIC RESEARCH GOALS

One of the easiest ways to stay organized and on track while researching ancestry is to focus on just one or two surnames at a time. While it's tempting to start on more surnames, refrain until you feel confident you have completed work on the lineages you've been actively researching. Obviously, the more surnames and placenames you research, the bigger your paper trail will become—making good organization necessary for continued and productive research.

KEEP IT SIMPLE AND FLEXIBLE

Good organizational systems are simple and allow you to find things quickly. Arrange your families in alphabetical order or use different colored folders to put everything in one polypropylene sleeve. Some genealogists like to use the numbers assigned in their genealogical software package. There is no universal way to organize—personalize your system to suit your style. Decide what works for you and stick with it. Just make sure it's simple enough for anyone to understand and allows for expansion when needed.

USE THE PROPER SUPPLIES

Save your genealogical research materials for the future by using acid- and lignin-free folders, polypropylene or Mylar enclosures and reinforced boxes available from specialty, scrapbook or art supply stores. Researching your family is an investment of time and money so preserve those resources by caring for your collection.

WORKING FILES VS. COLLECTIBLES

Photocopy all documents that you receive throughout your research to use in your scrapbook, keeping one copy intact for archival purposes. File your copies and scrapbook supplies earmarked for a page layout separate from originals. Note the exact location of the original on the back of the copies. Separate items such as acidic newspaper clippings and memorabilia from old photographs because the acid and ink could damage the pictures. Acid- and lignin-free paper or polypropylene sleeves can act as a buffer when a variety of genealogical materials are in the same storage container.

Genealogy Transformed: Turning Historical Data Into Stunning Scrapbook Pages

At some point in your ancestral research, you will feel that the time has come to begin creating family tree scrapbook pages. Creating a family tree scrapbook page is no different nor more difficult than making any other scrapbook page. If you've done your genealogical research, making the page is the easy part! Typically, you will find that you have plenty of document copies, heritage photos and journaling to corral neatly onto a page or a spread. Leave room in your page design for as much genealogical journaling as possible to eliminate any guesswork for your descendants. Help your research and presentation last for generations with archival-safe products. Look for acid- and lignin-free albums and papers, photo-safe adhesives and PVC-free page protectors and memorabilia pockets to hold precious keepsakes.

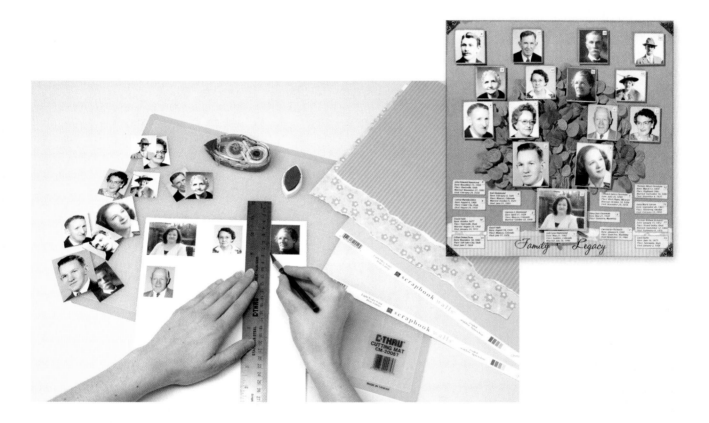

BASIC SCRAPBOOK TOOLS & SUPPLIES

- Archival-quality albums

- PVC-free page protectors

- Acid- and lignin-free papers

- Acid-free and photo-safe adhesives

- Pigment-ink pens and markers

- PVC-free memorabilia keepers, sleeves or envelopes

- Flat, photo-safe embellishments

- De-acidifying spray for news clippings or documents

HOW TO MAKE A FAMILY TREE SCRAPBOOK PAGE

Simply gather your materials, put them in order and then browse through this book for a few possible page designs that fit your needs and the materials you have. Select a background paper that pulls color from or complements your photos. Papers need not be all browns and dark colors unless that is your personal preference; experiment with color for an unexpected design surprise! Select page additions. Loosely assemble photos, title, journaling, memorabilia and page accents on layout paper and move them around for visual appeal. Trim and mat photos, then mount in place with adhesive. Add title and journaling. Complete the page with handmade or purchased page additions or accents. For instructions on how to replicate the page shown here and on page 1, see page 110.

Traditional Trees

The tree as a symbol of life and family descends from Old Testament religious symbolism. In young America, decorated family records appeared in New England's school and household art around the time of the American Revolution. In scrapbooking, a traditional family tree is a scrapbook page or spread that features a handmade tree complete with branches, leaves, photos—if you have them—and genealogical information. Creating a family tree may sound like a lot of work, but it doesn't have to be. If you've already done your ancestry homework, putting together a unique family tree is fun and easy!

Family tree page designs can include everything from conventional or whimsical trees to those that are sophisticated or simple. Some scrapbookers take the tree quite literally, featuring an actual photo of a physical tree as a backdrop for their family history.

In this chapter, you'll find many clever family trees made with products you may already have—such as silk and skeleton leaves, paper scraps, brads, mini frames, twine, chalk, wire and fibers. Experiment with basic quilling, photo mosaic, painting, stenciling, punch and embossing techniques to show off your research in style.

Whether you have enough information for just one family tree or a 12-generation forest, simply gather your roots, go out on a limb and grow an eye-pleasing visual remembrance of your ancestry that will please and educate for generations.

Lisa Dixon, East Brunswick, New Jersey, 2004 Memory Makers Master; See page 110.

- My mother
Ruth Dekker, 1911

- My family
Tuscaloosa, Alabama; 1947

remember
and *Cherish*

Christmas Card photo
Me and my brother Karl, 1940

Remember and Cherish

MAKE IT SIMPLE WITH A FAMILY TREE KIT

Assemble a four-generation family tree in minutes
with C-Thru Ruler's Family Tree kit. Write ancestors'
names on pre-made oval tags; mount on tree patterned paper. Embellish with ruler sticker. For left
page, layer torn green patterned paper with ivory
patterned paper on parchment background. Mat
two photos with brown and green patterned papers;
layer with silhouette cut photo and ruler stickers.
Rub on word transfer for title. Journal on parchment; attach journaling strips with small brads.

*Kathryn Chambless & Lori Pieper for C-Thru Ruler
Company*

*patterned papers (Anna Griffin, C-Thru Ruler, 7 Gypsies); ruler
stickers (EK Success); pre-made oval tags (C-Thru Ruler); rub-on
letters/word (Making Memories); brads*

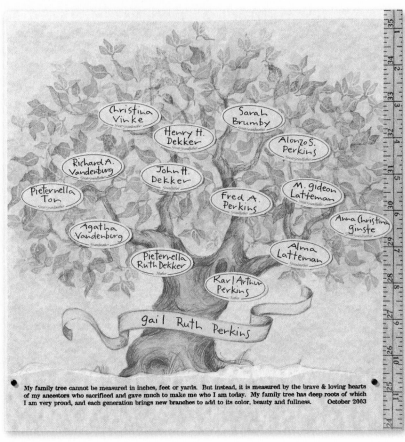

Christina Vinke
Great-Grandmother

Sarah Brumby
Great-Grandmother

Henry H. Dekker
Great-Grandfather

Alonzo S. Perkins
Great-Grandfather

Richard A. Vandenburg
Great-Grandfather

John H. Dekker
Grandfather

M. Gideon Latteman
Great-Grandfather

Pieternella Ton
Great-Grandmother

Fred A. Perkins
Grandfather

Anna Christina ginste
Great-Grandmother

Agatha Vandenburg
Grandmother

Alma Latteman
Grandmother

Pieternella Ruth Dekker
Mother

Karl Arthur Perkins
Father

gail Ruth Perkins

My family tree cannot be measured in inches, feet or yards. But instead, it is measured by the brave & loving hearts
of my ancestors who sacrificed and gave much to make me who I am today. My family tree has deep roots of which
I am very proud, and each generation brings new branches to add to its color, beauty and fullness.   October 2003

Smith Family Tree

IDENTIFY ANCESTORS WITH SCANNED SIGNATURES

Vickie identifies five generations of ancestors with genealogy information and copies of personal signatures scanned from wills, marriage licenses and deeds. Print title, captions and genealogy information on ivory cardstock. Scan and print signatures from archived family documents on ivory cardstock; mount with printed genealogy information over patterned paper background.

Vickie Smith Stovall, Owensboro, Kentucky

patterned paper (Creative Imaginations); cream cardstock; black pen

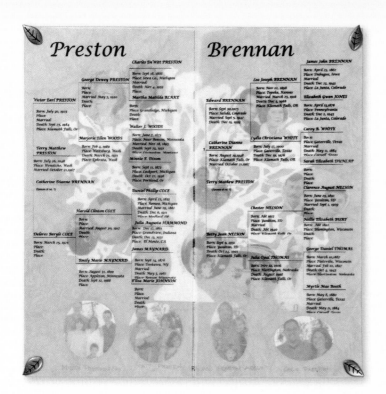

Preston-Brennan Family Tree

PRINT GENEALOGY ON SPACE-SAVING OVERLAY

Misty saves space by gathering six generations underneath a printed vellum overlay. Hand cut tree from white cardstock using a craft knife. Crop photos into circles and ovals; layer over tree and along bottom of patterned paper background. Print family pedigree charts on vellum; layer over background. Attach leaf eyelets at corners.

Misty Fox, Salem, Oregon

patterned paper (Anna Griffin); metal leaf eyelets (Making Memories)

Tracing the Family Tree

ASSEMBLE A PATTERNED PAPER TREE

Joy adds charm to her layered patterned paper tree with hand-stitched details. Tear green patterned paper for tree leaves. Cut tree trunk and branches from brown patterned paper; cut grass from multicolored patterned paper. Layer together on blue patterned-paper background. Print journaling and genealogy information on tan cardstock; shade with chalk. Attach eyelets to journaling; "hang" from tree with wire. Mount genealogy information on tree with small copper brads. Hand stitch buttons, flower stems and buttons with embroidery thread.

Joy Candrian, Sandy, Utah

patterned papers (Bo-Bunny Press, Karen Foster Design); brads; buttons; eyelets; wire; chalk; embroidery floss

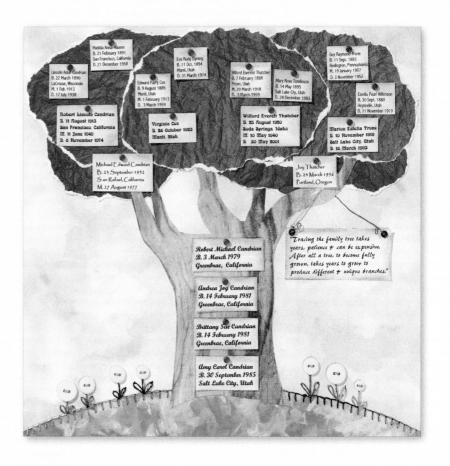

A Fairytale Family

CRAFT A WHIMSICAL APPROACH

April recalls a favorite family legend with fairies floating amongst the branches of a dimensional, paper-crafted tree. Paint background with watercolors on watercolor paper. Freehand cut tree shape from brown cardstock. Layer small brown cardstock pieces over trunk and branches for dimension. Die cut leaves from green cardstock; chalk for dimension and layer with foam tape. Print journaling and family names on vellum; tear edges. Emboss torn edges with gold embossing powder. Layer pre-made fairies and family names amongst tree leaves. Make tree swing from wood-grain cardstock strip and fibers tied around tree branch; weave silk flowers around fibers. Integrate fairy with swing. Mount paper grass along bottom of page.

April Nowotny, Bradenton, Florida

die-cut leaves (QuicKutz); fairies (Mamelok Press); gold embossing powder; fibers; watercolors; chalks; foam tape; wood-grain paper; flowers; paper grass

Kirkman Family Tree

MAKE A LIGHTHEARTED TREE

Sue likens her close-knit family to that of a well-tended garden that is nurtured to grow and blossom. Print title, journaling and family information on white cardstock. Hand cut title and trees using a craft knife; "carve" family name in tree trunk. Layer trees, title, matted photos, and small punched hearts on patterned paper matted with burgundy cardstock. Cut family information into hearts; shade with colored chalks. Punch edges of journaling with heart border punch. Silhouette cut flower from patterned paper.

Sue Little, Poplar Bluff, Missouri; Photos: Marshall Photography Arts, Cape Girardeau, Missouri

patterned paper (Hot Off The Press); heart border punch (Fiskars); small heart punch

Hannah's Roots

QUILL ANCESTRAL ROOTS

Quilling adds dimensional definition and elegance to Cherie's family tree. Cut silver metallic paper into scalloped design; layer with light blue border strips on blue cardstock background. Cut tree trunk and quilling strips from brown metallic paper. Mount quilled strips as branches and roots with a quick-drying adhesive. Cut leaves from green textured paper; chalk and crumple each leaf before mounting. Print family names and title words on metallic and colored vellums. Cut names into ribbon shapes. Crop the first title word into a tag using a template. Punch flower and layer over photo and gold tag. Silhouette cut large title word; add glitter glue. Cut two sizes of tags from silver and gold metallic papers using template. Mount photos on silver tags. Print genealogy information on vellum; mount on gold tags. Embellish gold tags with flowers made from layered punched shapes and jewels. Slice a vertical slit in large silver tags; slide gold tags in slit and mount on borders as shown.

Cherie Parker, London, Ontario, Canada

metallic papers (Scrapbook Sally); tag template (Provo Craft); leaf punch (Punch Bunch); flower punch (EK Success); sun punch (Marvy); faux jewels; glitter glue

A New Tree

DOCUMENT SIMILARITIES WITH PAPER DOLLS

Sarah features the male family resemblance amongst her husband's newly found brothers with custom details added to pre-made paper dolls. Freehand cut tree from solid and patterned papers; mat "branches" on green cardstock and layer over patterned background paper. Assemble paper dolls; detail with chalk, custom hairstyles and dimensional embellishments. Print journaling, photo captions and family names on vellum and green patterned paper. Mat die-cut title letters on vellum; layer with matted photos. Mat journaling and photo captions; attach with eyelets. Embellish with leaf stickers. Mat family names on yellow patterned paper; attach with heart brads.

Sarah Castro, Sacramento, California

patterned paper (Creative Imaginations); leaf stickers, paper dolls and velvet bow tie (EK Success); die-cut letters (Accu-Cut); eyelets; heart brads

Our Family

SIMPLIFY LAYOUT WITH FOLD-OUT PANELS

Cynthia assembles a large amount of ancestral information while keeping her layout from looking cluttered with simple fold-out panels. On left page, tear custom-made background paper; assemble and layer in tree shape on green cardstock background. Size, frame and print photos using image-editing software. Mat a succession of small photos on cream cardstock. Vertically score and fold embossed vellum ½" from left side; mount ½" flap behind cardstock background to create overlay. Print title and genealogy information with borders on clear vellum; crop and mount on embossed vellum over corresponding photo. Slice out window; frame and create ancestral lines with raffia strips. On right page, mat photos and printed poem on green patterned paper as shown. Mount photos matted on tan patterned paper on front of folded ivory cardstock; mount printed ancestors' names, scanned images and newspaper articles inside fold-outs. Print family names and directive text onto green embossed vellum and silhouette-cut leaves. Scatter both pages with leaves cut from custom-made paper.

Cynthia Schrauben, Mount Pleasant, Michigan

patterned papers (Colorbōk, DMD, Provo Craft); embossed vellums (K & Company); raffia

Kaegi

TEAR A SOFT, TEXTURED TREE

The gauzy texture of layered Japanese mulberry paper adds visual interest and dimension to Joy's family tree. Heat emboss silver frames/tags and mesh with copper embossing powder; set aside. Wrap embossed mesh across bottom of orange cardstock background. Layer torn Japanese paper with fibers and springroll paper for tree; shade springroll paper with brown chalk. Silhouette cut two photos; layer balance of photos behind preprinted frames. Die cut two sets of title letters from black cardstock; emboss one set with copper embossing powder before layering. Print genealogy information on vellum; mount behind embossed metal tags. Attach eyelets.

Anna Kaegi, Jacksonville, Florida

patterned paper; preprinted frames (Frances Meyer); metal frames/tags (Making Memories); springroll and mulberry paper (Pulsar); die-cut letters (QuicKutz); copper embossing powder; eyelets; chalk; fibers

The Tucker Tree

DANGLE FRAMES FROM BRANCHES

Denise adds a decorative element to family photos with a variety of scanned and re-sized frame designs. Mat patterned paper strip for border; vertically mount on matted patterned paper background. String gingham ribbon on buckle; attach cross charm with jump ring. Freehand cut sturdy base for tree from cardstock; cover with crumpled and flattened patterned paper. Shade with metallic rub-ons; mount with foam spacers. Scan and re-size photo frames; layer with photos and mount with foam spacers. Print text on white patterned paper and transparency. Slice windows in distressed and painted metal sheets; carefully roll edges with fingers. Mount frames over printed text. Emboss text on transparency with black embossing powder. Adhere letter stickers on metal disks for title; coat with crystal lacquer and let dry. Mount with foam spacers.

Denise Tucker, Versailles, Indiana, 2004 Memory Makers Master; Inspired by Jeniece Higgins, Lake Forest, Illinois; Photos: The Picture People, Florence, Kentucky

patterned paper (7 Gypsies, Anna Griffin, Karen Foster Design, Scrap Ease); metallic rub-ons (Craf-T); ribbon; ribbon buckle (Offray); cross charm (Beadery); metal sheets (Once Upon a Scribble); acrylic paint (Delta); round disks (Rollabind); letter stickers (EK Success); crystal lacquer (Plaid); photo frames (Making Memories); transparency

My Family Tree

HANG OLD-FASHIONED SIGNS

Lightweight and flexible model airplane balsa wood is the material of choice for Teri's old-fashioned hanging signs. This flexible yet sturdy wood can be stained, stamped and easily cut into shapes. However, make sure to treat wood with de-acidifying agent before placing next to photos. Stamp ancestor names and mount printed dates on wood strips; attach eyelets. Attach wood pieces together with wire; feed hemp string through eyelets and knot ends. Slice enlarged photo into 1" squares using mosaic template; assemble on green cardstock background. Hang signs from small brads; mount matted photos as shown. Stamp title at bottom of page.

Teri Lindsey, Fort Salonga, New York

patterned paper (Paper Patch); mosaic template (Wish in the Wind); letter stamps (Hero Arts); eyelets (Making Memories); wire; mini brads; hemp string; model airplane plywood

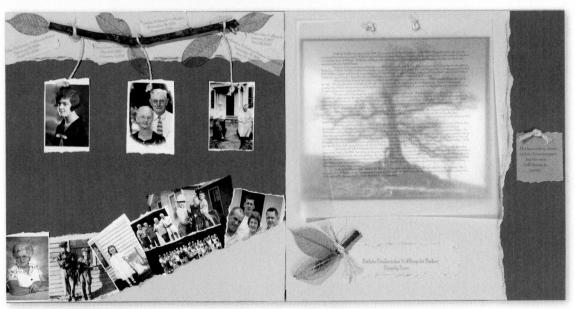

Esther Fredericka Vollbracht Baker

USE A REAL TREE PHOTO AND AN ACTUAL TREE BRANCH

Shawn features a branch of her family tree that dates back to 1851 with heritage photos dangling from a twig and skeleton leaf border. Tear tan cardstock borders; chalk edges before mounting on brown cardstock background. Print title, journaling, family information and quote on vellum. Layer journaling over large matted photo; secure with knotted twine strung through punched holes. Tear and chalk edges of title, family information and quote; embellish title and quote with twine, twig and skeleton leaves. Layer family information with skeleton leaves along top of left border; mount twig with glue dots. Tear photo edges. Dangle photos from twig with twine; feed through small punched holes and secure on back of page. String other end of twine through punched photo holes and knot. Layer balance of photos under torn cardstock corner.

Shawn Baker, Maywood, Missouri

skeleton leaves (Graphic Products Corp.); chalk; twigs; twine

My Family Tree

COMBINE TWIGS AND SKELETONIZED LEAVES

Branches from Joy's family tree dangle two-sided tags embellished with family photos and corresponding genealogy information. Tear edges of patterned paper; curl with fingers and rub with metallic rub-ons before matting on patterned cardstock. Mount skeleton leaves; layer heritage stickers and coat with crystal lacquer. Color tags with metallic rub-ons and chalk before wrapping edges with copper foil. Print genealogy information on ivory cardstock; mount on one side of tag and photo on backside. Tie tags with string; loop family name strip before dangling from twig. Mount twigs amongst leaves with glue dots.

Joy Candrian, Sandy, Utah; Photos: Leo Thatcher, Canby, Oregon

patterned papers and heritage stickers (Karen Foster Design); metallic rub-ons (Craf-T); skeleton leaves (Nature's Handmade Paper); tags (Avery); chalk; copper foil; crystal lacquer; brad; string

Family Love

DANGLE A "CHARM-ING" BRACELET

Jennifer combined her love of jewelry-making and scrapbooking with a genealogical "charm" bracelet. Stamp heart text, flowers, text and postage designs on ivory and pink cardstocks; heat emboss with silver or gold powders. Crop heart text into shape; tear around floral designs. Stamp ivory tag with family name; layer with floral tag and vellum flower and tie with pink yarn. Adhere letter stickers on metal-rimmed heart tag. Mat small flower cards on green cardstock; punch hole and tie with sheer pink ribbon. Collage tags, stamped designs, postage, coin and clock stickers, embossed vellum flowers, letter stickers and poem stone with torn patterned paper on ivory patterned cardstock. String letter tag stickers on sheer ribbon; secure to page with swirl clips. Print second family name and quote on gray cardstock. Cut name into tag shape; adhere clock sticker to tag and punch hole. Attach to swirl clip with wire. Tear around quote; mat on torn patterned paper. Layer torn patterned vellum over matted quote; punch small holes and tie with pink yarn. Create "bracelet" from linked jewelry jump rings; attach clasp. Mount photos to metal-rimmed tags. Adhere locket stickers to folded cardstock; silhouette-cut around right side of shape. Write genealogy information inside locket; punch small hole and attach jump ring. Embellish bracelet with photo tags, locket stickers and silver charms. Reinforce twig sticker by adhering to cardstock scrap; silhouette cut. String and drape charm bracelet on twig as shown.

Jennifer Guyor-Jowett, Saranac, Michigan

patterned papers (7 Gypsies, Anna Griffin); heart stamp (Hero Arts); hydrangea and postage stamps (Stampa Rosa); floral card, postage and letter stickers (EK Success); clock and locket stickers (NRN Designs); twig and coin stickers (Karen Foster Design); poem stone and large metal-rimmed heart (Creative Imaginations); tags (JudiKins, Making Memories); embossed vellum flowers (K & Company); swirl clips; sheer ribbon; pink yarn; die-cut heart; clock face; silver embossing powder

George Bradshaw (13)
Bessie Mae (Stevens) Bradshaw (14)
Children: Lorraine, (14) Georgia, (14) Dallas, (14) Myrtle, (14)

Eugene Carl Vetten (9)
Toni (Haukamp) Vetten (9)
Children: Eugenia (10), Anna (10) Walter (10)

Walter William Vetten (1)
Linda Lee (Roberts)Vetten (2)
Children: Andrea (3), Eugene (4), Lee (5)

George Leander Roberts (6)
Myrtle Lyn (Bradshaw) Roberts (6)
Children: Bobby,(7) Shirley, Betty, Linda (8)

William Vetten (11)
Anna (Oberheide) Vetten (11)
Children: Eugene, (12) William (12)

Tree of Life

APPLIQUÉ A FABRIC TREE

Andrea pieces coordinating fabrics together into a beautiful tree and background design using appliqué stitching techniques. Photocopy and size tree pattern on page 109. Transfer pattern onto freezer paper; cut out pieces and iron freezer paper shiny side down to front of fabric. Cut around pattern pieces and peel off freezer paper. Assemble into design; mount with iron-on fusible web. "Applique" design by machine stitching around each piece of background fabric with a tight zigzag stitch; hand stitch around tree trunk, branches and leaves. Scan, re-size and print photos to fit watch crystals; punch photos into circles before mounting inside watch crystals. Print numbered genealogy information on green cardstock; mat. Print and punch coordinating numbers from light green paper. Die cut title letters from green cardstock. Embellish title, genealogy information and tree with leaf buttons. Add satin ribbon corners to background cardstock; mat on dark green cardstock.

Andrea Lyn Vetten-Marley, Aurora, Colorado; 2004 Memory Makers Master

pattern on page 109; fabric (Marcus Brothers Textiles, Cranston); watch crystals (Magic Scraps, Scrapworks); die-cut letters (QuicKutz); satin ribbon corners (Colorbök); buttons (Jesse James); embroidery floss; thread; freezer paper; iron-on fusible web; circle punch

Bruce-Maul-Kerns-Zimmerman

PAINT AN ANCESTRAL WINDOW ORNAMENT

Andrea took her family tree from the scrapbook album to the window for some ancestral illumination. Photocopy and enlarge the pattern on page 108 to desired size. Crop photos to match ovals on tree; mount in place on transparency with double-sided adhesive. Follow the steps below to first create "leading," also tracing around the photo edges with pewter paint, and then to colorize the tree. Finish with letter-sticker title and photo captions in gold paint pen.

Andrea Lyn Vetten-Marley, Aurora, Colorado; 2004 Memory Makers Master

pattern on page 108; roll of transparency film; translucent paints (Delta); removable artist's tape; small paintbrush; letter stickers (Colorbōk); gold paint pen

1 Tape transparency over pattern and secure with removable artist's tape. Trace over all pattern lines with liquid lead and allow to dry overnight.

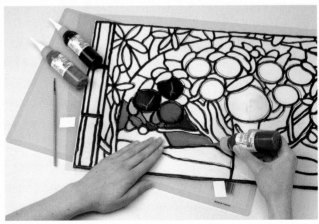

2 Fill in the spaces between liquid lead lines with jewel paints in desired colors. Use a small paintbrush to help spread color evenly. Allow project to dry overnight.

Wolf

FREEHAND DRAW AND PAINT A STORYBOOK TREE

Cara shows off her talent as a watercolor artist with a vibrant, hand-painted flower border and vine genealogy chart. Paint tree, flowers and vines with gouache watercolors on watercolor paper. Paint title letters with liquid gold-leaf paint. Handwrite genealogy information with brown ink; journal with pink ink. Mat hand-tinted photo on pink cardstock with torn edges; paint edges. Frame page with laser-cut border stickers layered over gold cardstock strips.

Cara Wolf-Vaughn, Carversville, Pennsylvania; Photo: Ruthe Vaughn, Alexandria, Virginia

metallic cardstock (Club Scrap); laser-cut border stickers (Mrs. Grossman's); watercolor paints

Our Family Tree

STENCIL AND STITCH AN HEIRLOOM

Heritage-rich stenciled colors and simple stitching give this page its homespun appeal. The page and page title are actually stenciled in vivid colors, but a pierced vellum overlay is used for stitching and to mute the colors to provide an age-old feel. Follow the steps below to re-create art. Finish art by adding handwritten ancestral names and rubbing outer page edges with brown paint or dye-based inkpad.

Barbara Swanson for American Traditional Designs, Northwood, New Hampshire

patterned vellum (EK Success); Tree of Life and Roman Calligraphy Alphabet stencils (American Traditional Designs); removable artist's tape and vellum adhesive (both 3M); yellow, red, green and brown stencil paints (American Traditional Designs); stenciling brush and palette; mouse pad or foam core board; piercing tool; embroidery thread; sewing needle and straight pins; buttons

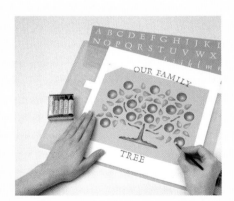

1 Secure tree stencil to center of background paper with removable artist's tape. Rub crayon-like paints onto palette. Dip brush into paint; swirl briskly onto a paper towel to remove excess paint. Tap or rub brush through stencil, using lighter colors first, then darker colors. Repeat process for page title.

2 Once paint is dry, use vellum adhesive to mount patterned vellum over background. Place art over mouse pad or foam core board; use piercing tool or sewing needle to pierce holes in a circular pattern around tree fruits.

3 Starting from the back of the art, begin stitching around a few of the fruits, inserting the needle on the top of the page when finished. Add straight pins and buttons in random fashion.

Our Tree, Our Roots

COLOR AND CROP A SWINGING TREE FAMILY

A brilliant artist in her own right, Samantha uses watercolor paper, gesso, Rapidiograph technical pens and watercolor paints to create a whimsical backdrop for her fun-loving family. For the artistic "faint of heart," you can use Samantha's original patterns and familiar scrapbooking supplies to replicate the art using your photos. First, photocopy or transfer the patterns on page 108 to cardstock in desired size. Scan and size photo subjects' heads to the same scale as the clothing patterns, silhouette-crop at neckline and set aside. Follow the steps below to create art; add cropped heads and journaling to swing art. Mat finished art, if desired.

Samantha Walker, Battle Ground, Washington

patterns on page 108; photocopier or transfer paper; watercolor pencils (Staedtler); blending brushes (EK Success)

1 Use colored pencils to color in and shade the tree using Samantha's original art colors as a guideline for pencil colors. Repeat the coloring process on the cardstock swings.

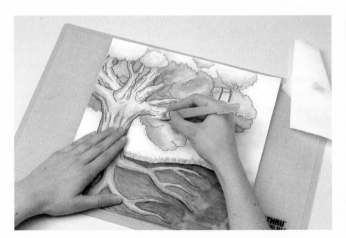

2 After coloring is completed, use blending brushes to lightly wash over water-colored pencil for a painterly effect. Use as little water as possible to prevent cardstock saturation, and clean tip of blender brush before tracing over a new color to discourage colors from bleeding together. Allow art to dry and iron art from back with dry iron on low setting or place under heavy books to flatten if needed.

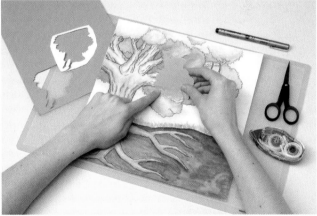

3 Trace cropped swing images onto additional cardstock; cut out traced images and mount on back of swing images for journaling. Silhouette-crop the swing images. Attach swing images to tree using additional water-colored tree boughs to hide seam.

Six Generation Family Tree

TIE PHOTO-LEAF CLUSTERS

Colleen ties together clusters of punched and embellished leaves along the branches of her family tree. Freehand cut tree branches from black cardstock; mount on patterned paper background. Select leaf shape for parental lineage. Assign each relative a color; punch leaves in shades of assigned color for ancestors' siblings. Embellish leaves with glitter glue. Paper piece acorns from brown cardstocks. Mount photos; adhere cameos on leaves for missing photos. Attach eyelets to background, punched leaves and acorns; tie leaf clusters to page with raffia. Print title and journaling on white cardstock; mount with embossed copper trim on yellow cardstock. Mount embossed copper leaves.

Colleen Burrs, Elk River, Minnesota

patterned papers (Provo Craft); oak and maple leaf punches (All Night Media, Marvy); glitter glue; eyelets; raffia; cameo; embossed copper leaves and border

Johnson-McMillan

LAYER PUNCHED PHOTO AND VELLUM LEAVES

Dori identifies her family's ancestors with punched vellum leaf overlays that slide to reveal a same-shaped and corresponding photo. Mount die-cut trees on patterned paper background. Punch photos and vellum with large oak and small fig leaf punches. Layer vellum and photo leaves and assemble on page; attach with small brads. Write corresponding family member name on vellum. Adhere letter stickers to metal-rimmed tags for title. String beads on wire; curl and shape before mounting as title and page embellishments.

Dori McMillan, Palisade, Minnesota

patterned papers (Scrap Ease); die-cut trees (Accu-Cut); oak and fig leaf punches (Emagination Crafts, McGill); metal-rimmed tags (Making Memories); letter stickers (Creative Imaginations); brads; wire; beads

As Time Goes By

EMBOSS EXTENDED TREE BRANCHES

Gail cleverly uses stamping and embossing to extend the branches of a tree die cut across a two-page spread and hidden photo and journaling panels. Mount patterned vellum sheets on white cardstock for strength; tape together on back with removable artist's tape. Shade die-cut tree with chalk; mount at center of two-page spread over seam. Use a metal ruler and craft knife to carefully slice the tree in half at seam of two-page spread. Use a metal ruler and craft knife to cut four same-size, gatefold panels and two single-folded panels. Follow the steps below to create the panels. Finish page with title, journaling, cropped photos and embellishments.

Gail Brown, Germantown, Wisconsin

patterned vellum (Worldwin); patterned papers (Daisy D's, NRN Designs); tree die cut (Deluxe Designs); leaf border edge punch (Fiskars); branch and leaf stamps (Stamps by Judith, Penny Black, respectively); charms and embellishments (Making Memories, found items); chalks; removable artist's tape; gold pigment ink; iridescent sparkle embossing powder; ribbon

1 Cover panels with patterned vellum, trimming to fit. Punch around panels' outer edges, re-punching part of each design for pattern consistency. Mount patterned papers of choice on panel interiors, trimming as needed to fit.

2 Mount the panels in place on background pages using original art for placement guidelines. Working in small sections at a time and starting at tree die cut, begin stamping branches and leaves in gold ink, extending across page spread and panel covers.

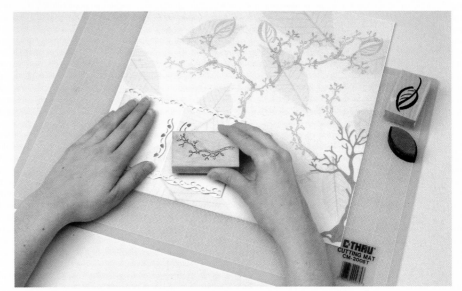

3 Sprinkle the inked designs with iridescent sparkle embossing powder. Gentle tap off any excess powder and set image with an embossing heat gun. Repeat steps 2 and 3 until two-page spread and closed panels are accented with tree branches and leaves. If desired, shade leaves with chalk.

Alla's Family Tree

TWIST A WIRE AND BUTTON TREE

Laurie shapes a dimensional family tree from braided and coiled wire branches embellished with decorative leaves. Follow the steps below for how to braid, wind and coil gold and black wire to create tree trunk and branches. Attach leaves to branches with wire; mount completed tree on patterned background paper. Mount flower buttons and leaves embellished with curled wire for borders. Print genealogy information on vellum; mat on ivory cardstock and mount decorative corners. Mat sepia-toned photos secured with clear photo corners on patterned papers. Mount laser-cut letters for title. String square letter beads on brown embroidery thread; stitch to page.

Laurie Nelson Capener, Providence, Utah

patterned papers (Carolee's Creations); wire; buttons (Jesse James); laser-cut letters (Provo Craft); square letter beads (Westrim); embroidery thread; flowers

1 To create tight spirals as featured on the page above, simply wrap wire around a small paintbrush. Loosen coils as needed for desired tendril lengths.

2 To create the wire filigree designs shown in the art above right, curl wire into heart, oval and spiral shapes, pinching the ends as needed to create points.

3 To create the tree featured in the art at the bottom of the next page, gather any number of 12" lengths of wire (the less wire, the thinner the tree; the more wire, the thicker the tree) and loosely wrap or braid the wires together to form trunk and separate wrapped sections toward the top to form tree branches.

Our Appalachian Family

Walter James Hysell   Margaret Elizabeth Spearhas   Lloyd Leslie Wetherholt   Ada Mae Coyle
Raymond Day Arnold   Mary Irene Maples   James Albert Hess   Flora Baxter Rice
Bobby Ray Arnold   Bonnie Gertrude Hysell   John William Hess   Charlotte Ann Wetherholt
Jeffrey Jon Arnold   Zane Curtis Arnold   Katherine Louise Hess

Our Appalachian Family

COAX WIRE INTO A FILIGREE TREE

Kathy re-creates a tree design from black fine-gauge wire that looks similar to the cast iron gates she remembers from her childhood home. Assemble tree from curved pieces of black fine gauge wire; stitch completed design to patterned vellum with black embroidery thread. Embellish with embossed leaves cut from patterned paper. Mat on green cardstock; tear edges and attach clear nails at corners. Mount on brown cardstock background. Mat photos on black cardstock; attach eyelets. Print title and family names on vellum; tear edges and mount with clear nails.

Kathy Arnold, Reynoldsburg, Ohio

patterned vellum (C-Thru Ruler); wire; clear nails (Chatterbox); embroidery thread; black eyelets

My Moore Family Tree

LOOSELY TWIST WIRE INTO TREE

Jenny softens a twisted wire formation with glistening floral die cuts and photo frames. Twist six sets of three or four 12" strands of wire. Bunch all wire sets together; twist bottom third for trunk. Shape top thirds of wire sets into branches as shown; mount with glue dots. Add glitter glue details to pre-made frames, tags and flower designs; let dry. Layer pre-made frames over photos with foam spacers. Print ancestors' names on lavender paper; cut into tag shape and string on silk ribbon. "Hang" from tree branches. Mount balance of framed photos and flower designs amongst branches.

Jenny Moore Lowe, Lafayette, Colorado

patterned papers (K & Company, Making Memories); wire; pre-made frames/tags (K & Company); lavender glitter; silk ribbon

Adams-Villa Family Tree

TORCH AN EMBOSSED METAL TREE

Stephanie's handcrafted tree emulates the forged metalwork of the Arts and Crafts Movement from primarily the late 1880s to 1920. Note that where ancestral photos were unavailable, she uses paper silhouettes—which can easily be replaced with newly acquired photos at a later date. Miniature frames add to the charm of this unique page. Follow the steps below to create tree and leaves in a well-ventilated area. Wear gloves, if desired. Extend the tree's branches with copper wire, securing on back with permanent adhesive; mount tree on page. Print title on transparency film; adhere. Print journaling on shrink plastic; follow manufacturer's instructions for shrinking and adhere. Suspend framed photos from wire and brads to complete page.

Stephanie Milner, Ventura, California

pattern on page 109; patterned paper (Pixie Press); light copper embossing metal (AMACO); leaf punch (Martha Stewart); inks (Jacquard Products); miniature frames (Card Connection, Impress Rubber Stamps); squirrel charm (Darice); copyright-free silhouettes clip art (Broderbund); inkjet shrink plastic (McGonigal); transparency film; copper and silver wire; mouse pad; brads

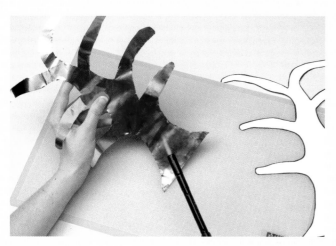

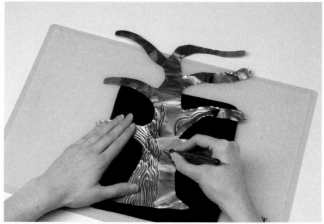

1 Size and photocopy tree pattern on page 109; trace around pattern onto metal. Cut out metal using old scissors or tin snips. Use a micro torch to colorize the metal tree, being careful not to hold metal too close to the portion being heated. If desired, practice first on a scrap of metal to determine the amount of time to heat the metal for the color you desire.

2 Place metal tree on a mouse pad and use an embossing stylus to freehand draw "bark" lines onto tree.

3 For richer color and more dimensional bark, rub brown ink over the tree with a soft cloth or your fingertip. Repeat steps 1, 2 and 3 using leaf punch, embossing stylus, micro torch and green ink to create leaves.

Gagne

DANGLE TAGS FROM FIBER BRANCHES

Johanna accents her family's European lineage with printed French text and free-flowing fibers that suggest the shape of a tree. Mount fibers for tree shape over patterned paper background with reposi-tional adhesive. Punch leaves from green vellum and white paper; layer vellum leaves along tree shape. Emboss remaining leaves with gold embossing powder; set aside. Lightly stain and ink tags with green and brown ink pads. Randomly press embossing pad on tags; heat emboss with gold embossing pow-der. Mount photos on tags; journal with metallic pen. Attach eyelets to tags; string on fibers as shown. Use liquid adhesive to mount fibers on page; secure tags. Stamp and emboss family name on vellum for title; mount behind gold decorative frame. Embellish title and tags with leaves punched from gold metal sheets and gold embossed leaves.

Johanna Peterson, El Cajon, California; Photos: Alpine Photo, Alpine, California

patterned papers (Creative Imaginations); fern and leaf punches (Punch Bunch); birch leaf punch (Family Treasures); tags (American Tag); rubber stamp letters (PSX Design); gold scrap metal (Once Upon A Scribble); gold embossing powder; eyelets; gold frame; fibers; metallic pen

BLUEPRINTS

grandma

mother

brother sister

father

grandpa

Gottlieb Hardt

Lydia Clauser Hardt

Edward Herman Oelke

Rosa Ebert Oelke

OTTO CASPER HARDT
B. 1-30-1920
CLINTON JUNCTION, WI
D. 12-30-1988
WASHBURN, WI

LORRAINE GLADYS ANDERSON
B.1-16-1918
D.5-5-1999
WASHBURN, WI

CAROLE JEAN HARDT
B.5-3-1944
ASHLAND, WI

ROBERT REUBEN OELKE
B.10-25-1943
EAU CLAIRE, WI

REUBEN EDWARD OELKE
B.7-4-1916
D.10-13-1994
EAU CLAIRE, WI

ROSA EBERT
D.1952

EDWARD HERMAN OELKE
B.1879
D.1952

AMELIA SENESE
B. 5-23-1882
OLIVETO CITRA, ITALY
D. 10-10-1954

ROMEO CAPPETTA
B. 7-20-1877
SALERNO, ITALY
D. 2-7-1942

FRIEDA MARY CAPPETTA
B. 1-19-1912
D.8-18-2003
FRANKFORT, IL

KRISTIN KAY OELKE
B.5-5-1969
WAUSAU, WI

NICHOLAS BENJAMIN
B.12-18-1993

VIVIAN LOUISE STANLEY
B.8-29-1938
CHICAGO, IL

JOHN ANTHONY CONTINO
B.5-8-1969
OAK LAWN, IL

SARAH HEALD
B. 12-12-1879
D. 1-14-1966

WALTER J. STANLEY
B. 3-18-1878
D. 1-17-1971

THOMAS JOSEPH CONTINO
B.6-16-1935
BRIDGEVIEW, IL

NANCY PALUMBO
B.8-31-1935
CHICAGO, IL

IDA LAMANTIA
B.1-24-1900
D. 5-7-1976

JOHN PALUMBO

MARY DAQUILA
B. 1892

JOSEPH F. CONTINO
B. 1903
D. 6-9-1979

THOMAS SALVATORE CONTINO
B. 8-28-1913
BEAVER FALLS, PA
D. 3-7-1986
CHICAGO, IL

Pedigree Charts

Genealogical research is a labor of love that results in a lot of family names, dates and place names. A pedigree chart provides a valuable way to present your historical family information for posterity in a format that is easily understandable. A pedigree chart shows the lines of your direct ancestors, beginning with you or your children and reaches back through time as far as research allows.

Pedigree charts have been created and used for centuries by families around the world. Pedigree charts can be simple and basic or quite elaborate. They can be generated with your computer and genealogy software, downloaded from the Internet or handmade. Some pedigree charts have photos, while others do not. Some pedigrees are very structured, while others are more freestyle. Finally, pedigree charts can look very authoritative and historic or colorful, contemporary and playful. The one thing all pedigree charts have in common is sound historical family information.

A completed pedigree chart is one of the crowning glories of genealogical research— a visual record of ties that bind. Pedigree charts always make a handsome statement in a scrapbook album, or you might find that you love yours so much that you frame it for permanent display!

Kristin Contino, Milwaukee, Wisconsin. See page 110.

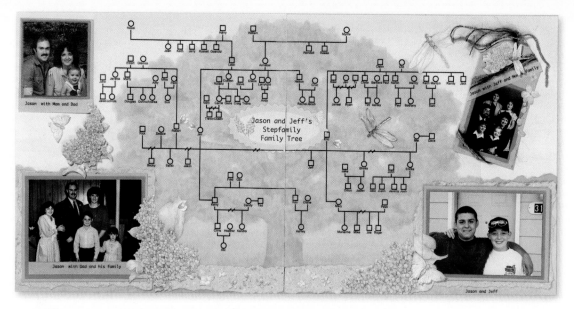

Jason and Jeff's Stepfamily Family Tree

HONOR A BLENDED FAMILY

Jenny unites both sides of her sons' blended family on a comprehensive diagrammatic family tree chart that maps patterns and relationships with symbols called a genogram. Print genogram on vellum; mount over patterned paper background. Print title, photo captions and journaling on vellum, sticker frame and patterned papers. Layer blue cardstock tag with photo, torn purple cardstock and pre-made die cuts and stickers. Mount vellum photo caption; wrap and tie with fibers. Double mat three photos on purple and blue cardstocks embellished with glitter glue; mount one photo on folded blue cardstock for hidden journaling. Mount printed journaling inside folded cardstock. Layer handmade paper and pre-made die cuts along bottom of page and around matted photos.

Jenny Moore Lowe, Lafayette, Colorado

patterned papers (Making Memories, Sandylion); die cuts and frames (K & Company); fibers (Magic Scraps); glitter glue (Stampendous); suede paper

My Birthstone Tree

EMBELLISH FAMILY CHART WITH BIRTHSTONES

Jenny presents a colorful, six-generation family chart using "birthstone" jewels to represent ancestors' birth dates. Print generational fan chart using computer software. Silhouette tree trunk from patterned paper; layer with printed fan chart on patterned background paper. Mount jewel "birthstones" that correspond with each ancestor's birth date. Embellish punched leaves, pre-made die cuts and stickers with glitter glue; let dry before layering along bottom of page and around fan chart. Add dimension to layers with foam spacers. Slice branches from large tree stickers; reassemble in desired position over fan chart with silk ribbon. Mount punched and glittered leaves. Crop photos into circles; mount on die cuts. Print chart captions and title on vellum; layer over ribbon and along flower border at bottom of page.

Jenny Moore Lowe, Lafayette, Colorado

patterned paper (Colorbōk); flower stickers and pre-made die cuts (K & Company); Reunion software (Leister Productions); tree sticker (EK Success); glitter glue (Stampendous); silk ribbon; faux jewels; leaf punch

Weller Pieces of Family

PIECE TOGETHER FAMILY HISTORY

Debbie's love of working on jigsaw puzzles inspired her to piece together genealogical information about four generations of a close-knit family. Print genealogy information on patterned papers; cut into puzzle pieces using stencil. Arrange as desired. Die cut title letters from solid and patterned cardstocks.

Debbie Weller, Kalispell, Montana

patterned paper and puzzle template (Club Scrap); die-cut letters (Sizzix)

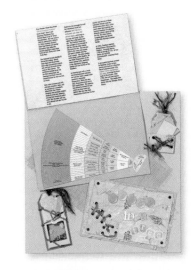

Penelope Stout Lives in a Tree

MEMORIALIZE AN INVINCIBLE ANCESTOR

Jenny presents a lovely tribute to a courageous ancestor from which the phrase "stout-hearted woman" was coined. Layer foldout flap for hidden genealogy chart and family history with torn and distressed patterned and embossed papers; attach eyelets. Embellish colored cardstock strips with eyelets, fibers and gold charm. Create medallion with color-copied images mounted on circle cut from thin aluminum sheet; punch hole and tie with fibers. Print fan-shaped genealogy chart and family history; mount inside folded cardstock. Tear corner of distressed patterned paper; attach eyelets and lace with fibers. Layer with torn handmade paper on blue cardstock; attach eyelets at corners. Layer with mesh on lavender background cardstock. Assemble title from metal, sticker and pebble letters. Cut tags from colored cardstocks in a variety of sizes. Punch square in one tag for shaker box window; mount transparency and fill shaker box with torn cardstock, heart charms and beads before sealing with foam tape. Layer tags and collage with handmade and distressed papers; punch hole at top. Tie and wrap with fibers; add heart charm. Layer handmade, colored and patterned papers on smaller tag. Attach eyelets; add fibers and heart charm.

Jenny Moore Lowe, Lafayette, Colorado

patterned papers (K & Company, Making Memories); letter stickers and poem stones (Creative Imaginations); metal letters (Making Memories); aluminum (AMACO); eyelets; fibers; square punch; suede paper; mesh; handmade paper; gold heart charms; beads

My Royal Tree and Me

UNFOLD ROYAL TIES

Jenny wraps up a long line of ancestral history under a fold-out panel that reveals ties to 13 kings, a queen, a saint, and over 21 U.S. Presidents. Layer patterned vellum over patterned background paper. Print parallel descendant tree, photos and family history on white paper using family tree software; piece together to make one long page. Accordion fold; mount patterned vellum for cover. Create closure for fold-out panel; secure ribbon and fibers under large jewel. Mount second large jewel on outside of fold-out flap as shown; wrap fibers around jewels. Print title on vellum; color inside letters with gold leafing pen. Fashion large crown from printed clip art crown painted gold and purple; adorn with jewels, pearl trim and layer over red handmade paper. Slice patterned vellum along design lines; secure matted photo and foreign currency sticker into sliced area. Embellish page with remaining pre-made dimensional stickers.

Jenny Moore Lowe, Lafayette, Colorado

patterned papers (Karen Foster Design, NRN Designs); iridescent paints (Dr. Ph Martin); gold leafing pen (Krylon); stickers (EK Success); Reunion software (Leister Productions); fibers; faux jewels; pearls

Strong Family

RECORD A ROYAL CONNECTION

Angie discovered her ties to royalty after researching a handwritten document that contained information about relatives dating back to the early 1600s. Print and silhouette cut family crest; mount on patterned background paper. Create name banners using a template; calligraphy ancestors' names and dates. Mount banners and photos over vertical ribbon strands as shown. Tie two ribbon bows; mount above family crest.

Angie DeLuca, Orlando, Florida

patterned paper (Hot Off The Press); banner template (source unknown); ribbon

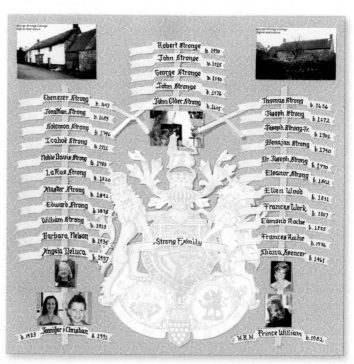

Ancestors of Kylie & Brendan

STITCH A PEDIGREE CHART

Stacy was once told "threads tie the family together," which gave her the idea of stitching the ancestor lines in her family tree. Double mat background patterned paper with green and purple cardstocks. Print genealogy information and title on ivory cardstock; mat on green cardstock and trim with decorative scissors. Place matted genealogy blocks on pages in desired position; draw connecting lines with pencil. Remove matted blocks; pierce holes along pencil lines with piercing tool to ensure even stitches. Stitch with green and purple embroidery thread to differentiate two sides of the family. Mount matted blocks with foam tape. Print journaling on vellum. Assemble flowers from shapes punched from purple papers; layer and mount at page corners.

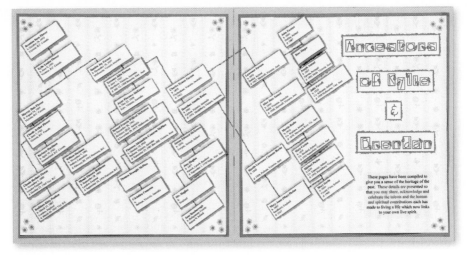

Sandra Flower, Victoria, British Columbia, Canada

patterned papers (K & Company); embroidery thread; small flower punch; small circle punch; decorative scissors; foam tape

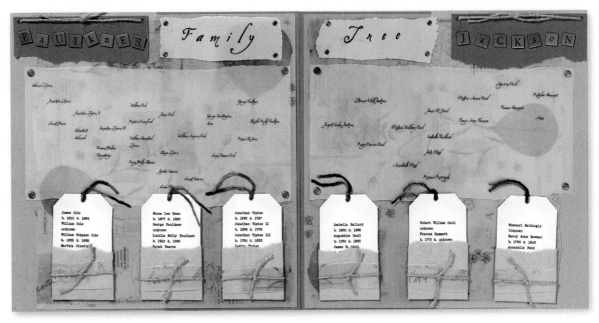

Faulkner-Jackson Family Tree

TUCK GENEALOGICAL TAGS INTO VELLUM POCKETS

Cherie simplified the design of a pedigree chart by eliminating lines and boxes and printing only the ancestors' names on the chart. She detailed genealogy information and dates on tags tucked in small torn and embellished brown bags. Mount patterned vellum with torn edges over brown cardstock background. Print title words and ancestors' names on vellum and genealogy information on ivory cardstock. Tear top and bottom edges of vellum with ancestors' names; mount with snaps. Tear vellum edges with title words; attach with eyelets. Complete title with metal letter tiles mounted on green cardstock strip; tear bottom edge. Attach to page with eyelets; string twine and tie. Cut genealogy information into tags; lightly shade with green ink pad. Attach eyelets and tie with fibers. Tear off top half of small brown bags; wrap with patterned vellum and tie with twine. Mount along bottom of pages; slip tags in bags.

Cherie Chavez, Peoria, Arizona

patterned vellum (Autumn Leaves); snaps, eyelets; letter tiles (Making Memories); small brown bags (DMD); twine; fibers

Parents & Grandparents

CROP THEN AND NOW PHOTO CHARMS

Mary Ann uses both sides of oval-cropped paper charms to feather then and now photos for her family tree. Crop all photos into ovals; mount on both sides of complementary-colored cardstock mats. Attach photo charms on page with ribbon bows. Print family history information on parchment or vellum, tear around edges and place beneath photos.

Mary Ann Watkins, Bradenton, Florida

patterned paper (Generations); complementary-colored cardstock; parchment paper or vellum; ribbon

The Circle of Life

ENCIRCLE A CHILD WITH BELOVED ANCESTORS

Misty surrounds her daughter with a matriarchal circle of women who have passed their quiet and unwavering strength on through the generations. Alter color of scanned photos with image-editing software; crop into same-sized circles. Assemble in circles on patterned paper background as shown. Print title, genealogy information and quote on vellum; tear edges. Mat on burgundy mulberry paper.

Misty Fox, Salem, Oregon

patterned paper (Creative Imaginations); mulberry paper; image-editing software

Our Heritage, Our Future

INTERMINGLE PHOTOS AND GENEALOGY IN UNIFORM SQUARES

Liz assembled a four-generation family tree with rows of ancestral information and over 50 photos. Print genealogy information on ivory cardstock. Punch photos and printed information into squares; shade male squares with brown chalk and female squares with pink chalk. Assemble on yellow cardstock in generational rows, beginning with oldest ancestors. Cross-stitch squares of married couples with tan embroidery thread; embellish with stitched heart buttons. Assemble second row with next generation; connect married family members with curled wire and punched heart embellishment. Continue rows with information and photos of subsequent generations until present. When family tree is complete, double mat on green and ivory cardstocks. Hand cut title from ivory cardstock. Curl wire into border design; embellish with punched metal hearts.

Liz Davidson, Welwyn Garden City, England

square punch; embroidery thread; heart buttons; wire; heart punch

My Heritage

STITCH A PATCHWORK PEDIGREE

Darla pieced together a "love" quilt that documents marriage information about four generations of husbands and wives. Print title, family name and genealogy information on patterned papers. Crop photos, title and patterned paper into heart shapes using a template. Mount heart-shaped photos on floral and pink patterned paper squares. Cut green patterned paper rectangles, large and small patterned paper triangles, and printed genealogy information according to quilt templates. Layer and piece together shapes for quilt design. Border page with green patterned paper strips and pink page corners. Draw stitching lines with black pen.

Darla Richard, Waynesburg, Ohio

patterned papers (Anna Griffin, Hot Off The Press); quilt template

Jane's Legacy

FEATURE A NAMING-TRADITION PEDIGREE

Lisa displays a visual account and story behind the family tradition of passing on the name "Jane" for over 70 years. Layer patterned papers for background; stamp initial, script, flowers and border designs with brown ink. Print title twice on vellum and white cardstock; tear bottom edge of vellum and layer to create shadow. Staple to page over mesh and silver word sticker. Mount metal-rimmed vellum tag with written words over definition; staple transparency word and adhere flower sticker. Print genealogy information and photo caption on cardstock; mat direct family line on green cardstock and shade with chalk. Assemble genealogy chart; form ancestor lines with cardstock strips. Emboss edges of metal word tag; tie with ribbon. Rub white word transfer at top of right page. Single and double mat photos on pink and green cardstocks; tear bottom edge of single matted photos. Layer photos with em-bossed pewter sticker and mesh; embellish with dimensional flower stickers and round mirror tile. Layer painted metal word tag and word pebble on stamped decorative tag; attach brad over die-cut flowers. Journal on white cardstock; mat on green cardstock. Create embellishment from layered scalloped metal tile, punched and chalked cardstock square, stitched metal tile and letter pebble.

Lisa Jane Acciacca, Oceanside, California: Photos: Sears Portrait Studio, Carson, California & The Picture People, Carlsbad, California

patterned papers (Magenta); initial, script, flowers and border stamps (Close To My Heart, Inkadinkado, Rubber Stampede); mesh (Magic Mesh); definition (Foofala); flower stickers (EK Success, Magenta); embossed pewter sticker (Magenta); metal word tag, word and letter pebbles (Li'l Davis Designs); decorative tag, laser-cut flowers (Deluxe Designs); round mirror tile; ribbon; silver word sticker; stapler, metal-rimmed vellum tag, transparency word, rub-on word transfer; embossing powder; chalks; brad

Our Family Tree

LINK DOLLS IF NO ANCESTRAL PHOTOS

Jill turned her son's health history project into an informative family tree that traces hereditary diseases passed on from generation to generation. Mount colored cardstock strips on brown cardstock background. Create faces from punched circles, fibers and beads; draw facial features with brown pen. Assemble into family tree; mount fibers for ancestor lines. Create color-coded key with small squares punched from colored cardstocks. Write genealogy information with black pen. Adhere letter stickers for title; mat on cardstock and attach with eyelets.

Jill Gross, Roselle, Illinois

fibers; beads; letter stickers (Creative Imaginations); eyelets; large and small circle punches; large and small heart punches; small square punch

Our Heritage

DESIGNATE FAMILY LINES

Beth adds color and organization to the many names that make up her pedigree chart by assigning each family line a specific font and color. Triple mount large photo on green, mauve and burgundy cardstocks; punch corners of second mat with decorative corner punch. Double mat two photos; mount torn mulberry paper corners and layer over torn burgundy cardstock. Mount metal word plaques under photos. Attach metal letter eyelets for title on torn mulberry paper strip. Print genealogy information on ivory cardstock; layer under chalked vellum. Attach eyelets at top two corners and string with fibers. Hang from buttons mounted over skeleton leaves. On opposite page, print ancestors' names on colored cardstocks; cut to size and mat. Attach eyelets to focal names of descendant chart; tie together with fibers. Mount all names on patterned paper background. Attach metal letter and word eyelets on torn and layered mulberry paper and green cardstock tag; attach eyelet and tie with fibers.

Beth Phillips, Wausau, Wisconsin

patterned papers (Colorbök, Rocky Mountain Scrapbook); corner punch (Fiskars); buttons (Jesse James); skeleton leaves (All Night Media); metal word eyelets (Making Memories); metal word plaques (Darice); fibers

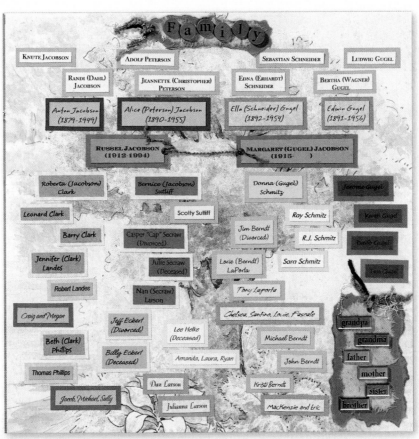

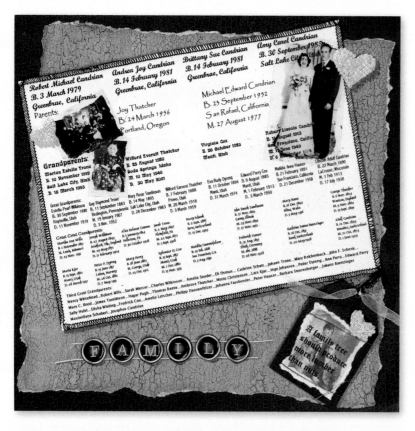

Candrian Family Tree

INCLUDE INFORMATION IN MINI BOOKS

When a vast amount of genealogical data presents a challenge when trying to fit it all on scrapbook pages, try Joy's solution of using mini booklets and a simple photo transfer process to condense information. Mount torn and chalked cardstock on patterned background. To create photo transfers, shrink and color copy photos and documents onto regular photocopy paper. Apply a laminate sheet to front, smoothing with a bone folder. Place laminated copy into warm water for a few minutes to absorb water; use bone folder to gently remove backing paper. Follow the steps at the bottom of page 51 to create mini booklets. Assemble photo transfers, mini booklets and title and journaling on vellum to finish page.

Joy Candrian, Sandy, Utah; Photos: Rick Norton, Palm Beach Gardens, Florida

patterned paper (Bo-Bunny Press); double-sided cardstock for booklets (source unknown); clear lacquer (Sakura Hobby Craft); laminate (C-Line); white vellum; chalk; ribbon; old buttons

My Mothers

FEATURE FEMININE ACCENTS

Chris gets in touch with the feminine side of her ancestral history with layers of vintage lace and detailed journaling about each woman's extraordinary life. Mount ivory patterned paper strips for border over green patterned paper background; vertically layer lace and decorative border stickers. Print journaling on white cardstock; trim with decorative scissors. Mat photos on white, ivory and pink cardstocks; trim white mats with decorative scissors. Layer large photos and printed journaling over lace trim. Stain tan cardstock with tea; cut into tags. Punch circles from brown cardstock; mount on tag and punch again with a hole punch. Tie with string; feed ends through flower shape punched on page and secure at back. Mount balance of matted photos and captions; adhere vintage-themed and flag stickers. Layer two sizes of squares punched from patterned paper and ivory cardstock; write letters on small squares for title.

Chris Olesen, Gardnerville, Nevada

patterned papers and vintage-themed and flag stickers (Creative Memories); lace; circle punch; square punch

1 Cut double-sided cardstock into 2" wide strips. You'll need 3 strips per booklet. Score and fold the strips accordion-style at 2" intervals; glue the 3 strips together on the backside of paper. Repeat for second booklet.

2 Rub fine-grained sandpaper along the front of folded strips to distress. Cut a piece of ¼" ribbon 2½" long and attach one end to the left side of the front cover behind the fold, gluing ribbon in between folds. For each book, cut a 2½" piece of elastic cord and tuck it so that it forms a loop onto the right side of front cover and the first page; attach with glue. Repeat with second booklet.

3 Stitch around covers 1/8" from edge, catching elastic cord in the stitching. Attach second end of ribbon to back covers, leaving about ¼" between the pages unglued. Glue the ribbon in between the last fold and the second-to-last fold. Apply a thin layer of glue along the cover and press to the next page. Place the booklets beneath something heavy for a few hours to press flat.

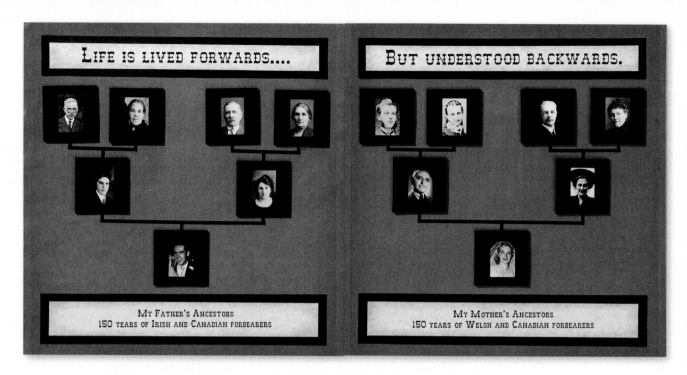

Life is Lived Forwards...But Understood Backwards

CREATE SLIDE MOUNT PHOTO BOOKLETS

Rachel uses acid-free black scrapbook pages with an extended binding edge to construct striking yet durable slide mount booklets. Cut fold-out panels for booklets from black scrapbook pages twice the width of slide mount, making sure to vertically center the binding edge before cutting. Fold on binding; layer and mount photo and slide frame on front of fold-out flap. Print title, genealogy information and journaling on parchment paper. Mount genealogy information inside frame booklets. Shade title and journaling with chalks; mat on black cardstock. Draw ancestral lines with pencil on brown cardstock background; adhere black sticker strips over penciled lines. Mount slide mount booklets; slice openings in page protector for covers to slip through.

Rachel Smith, Vancouver, British Columbia, Canada

patterned paper (Design Originals); black sticker strips (Creative Memories); paper slide mounts; chalks

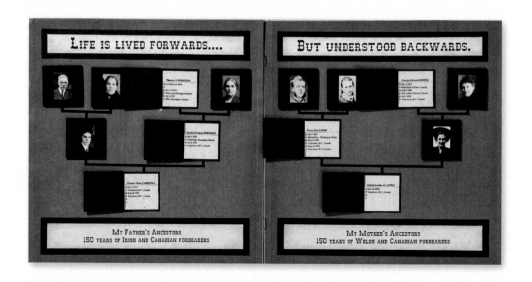

Family Tree

SCRAPBOOK A PHOTO PEDIGREE

Angie assembles a monochromatic family tree with fold-out photo cards that open up to reveal snippets of family history. Layer torn cardstock strips for borders over patterned paper background; shade with chalk and roll torn edges with fingers. Create fold-out photo cards that open up to reveal written family history from folded cardstock strips. Mount photos and genealogy information printed on vellum on front of cards; journal inside with metallic pens. Adhere word stickers for title on matted brown cardstock strip; hang from small brads with knotted jute string. Mount word pebbles on oval frames and watch crystal over watch parts. Tie jute string to keys; dangle from brad.

Angie Head, Friendswood, Texas; 2004 Memory Makers Master

patterned papers (Design Originals); pebble words and oval frames (Li'l Davis Designs); watch parts (7 Gypsies); watch crystal (Scrapworks); word stickers (Karen Foster Design); brads; jute string; chalk; keys

Brueck Brick

FEATURE ANCESTRY WITH A POSTAGE THEME

Large postage stamps chronicle MaryJo's Prussian roots and her ancestors' emigration from Germany to America. Layer torn patterned papers for background; chalk torn edges. Create "stamps" on computer using graphic design software with scanned photos and genealogy information. Trim with decorative scissors; mount over black cardstock strips. Create "postcard" journaling on computer; print on parchment paper and embellish with stamp sticker. Photocopy passenger list from book (*Germans to America, List of Passengers Arriving at U.S. Ports, Volume 2, May 1851 to June 1852*, 1988, by Ira A. Glazier and P. William Felby); mat on black cardstock. Layer postage stamp and postcard stickers, passenger list and original pen drawing with photo "stamps." Layer preprinted title letters; adhere second row with foam spacers.

MaryJo Regier, Memory Makers Books

patterned papers (K & Company, Karen Foster Design); pre-printed letters (Foofala); stamp and postcard stickers (Me & My Big Ideas); page design and image-editing softwares (QuarkXPress, Adobe Photoshop); decorative scissors (Fiskars)

Walter James Pharaoh

USE PAPER SILHOUETTES WHEN NO PHOTOS ARE AVAILABLE

Juli substitutes missing family member photos with silhouette clip art to complete the family tree that chronicles a legacy of extraordinary men on her father's side of the family. Scan, restore, size and frame photos using image-editing software. Mount framed photos and clip art silhouettes on tan cardstock; write genealogy information. Distress cardstock edges and balance of photos by scraping with a craft knife; shade with chalks. Layer matted photos with two colors of ribbon on handmade paper background. Mount torn and chalked vellum at bottom of handmade paper background; curl edges. Attach eyelets at bottom corners; mount photos. Write title and journaling on vellum; tear edges and roll with fingers. Mat title on chalked tan cardstock; attach with eyelets.

Juli Pomainville, Canton, New York

image-editing software (Adobe Photoshop); handmade paper; chalks; eyelets; clip art; ribbon

Our Family Tree

CREATE DEPTH WITH VELLUM OVERLAY

Aila cleverly prints her ancestral information on a vellum overlay, which also serves to soften the stickers behind it. Adhere vintage-themed stickers on patterned paper background. Single and double mat photos on black cardstock and torn mulberry paper. Print genealogy information on vellum. Adhere title and colored stickers.

Aila Lappalainen, Las Vegas, Nevada

patterned papers (Daisy D's); stickers (Colorbök, EK Success, NRN Designs)

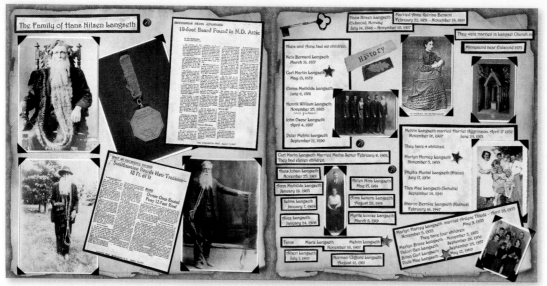

The Family of Hans Nilsen Langseth

INCORPORATE AN UNUSUAL FAMILY TALE

Vicki researched a family tale about a curious relative whose 19-foot beard earned him a place in the *Guinness Book of Records*. Print genealogy information on white cardstock; shade with chalk and mat on black cardstock. Layer photos, genealogy and photocopied information on patterned paper background; mount photos with black photo corners. Embellish with heritage stickers and gold star brads.

Vicki Clark, Lewiston, Minnesota

patterned papers and heritage stickers (Karen Foster Design); photo corners (Fiskars); star brads (Making Memories); chalks

My Ancestors

ASSEMBLE PAST HISTORY WITH PRESENT TECHNOLOGY

A layered multigenerational pedigree chart comes together in a snap with the help of a heritage scrapbooking kit that includes solid and patterned papers, themed embellishments and a computer program that simplifies the process of making descendant charts. Print journaling, scanned photos and genealogy information on light-colored cardstocks; mat and layer with pre-made title on patterned paper background as shown. Embellish with stained glass and buttons.

Kathryn Engemann for Heritage Hearts, Provo, Utah

Family Tree Software Kit (Heritage Hearts); stained-glass pieces; buttons

The Circle of Life

PIN UP AN ANCESTRAL CLOTHESLINE

Stephanie was inspired by a song's words to display a discovered bag of family photos as a round family tree. Print genealogy information on ivory cardstock and part of title and song words on vellum. Tear and chalk vellum edges of song; mount on patterned paper background with eyelets. Mat photos on white cardstock. Mount title words and matted photos on ivory cardstock with printed genealogy information; tear and chalk edges. Arch die-cut title letters across pages above and below featured family member. Surround title with ancestor information clipped to hemp string with decorative clothespins; include offshoots from circle to represent family lineage. Adhere text sticker on torn and chalked vellum strip.

Stephanie Ackerman, East Meadow, New York

patterned papers (Paper Loft); die-cut letters (Sizzix); clothespins (Card Connection); text sticker (Karen Foster Design); eyelets; chalks; hemp string

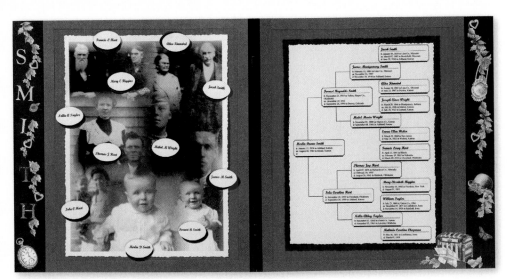

Smith Family Tree

BLEND IMAGES INTO A PHOTOMONTAGE

Image-editing software gives Lori the tools she needs to layer, soften and blend images together into a multigenerational photomontage. Triple mat photomontage and printed pedigree chart; trim mats with decorative scissors. Print family names on gray cardstock; cut into ovals and mat. Mount all on black scrapbook pages as shown; adhere letter and heritage stickers.

Lori Smith, Meade, Kansas

Family Tree Software (Family Tree Maker); image-editing software (Microsoft Picture It); heritage stickers (Creative Memories)

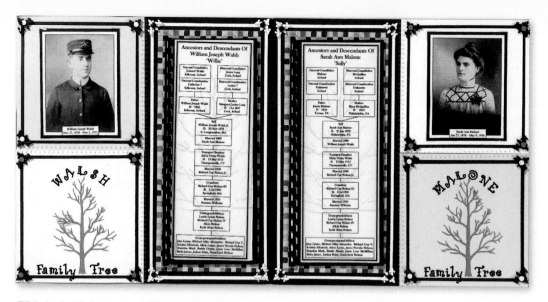

Walsh/Malone Family Trees

MAKE TWIN COMB-BOUND BOOKLETS

Third-prize Memory Makers' Family Tree Contest winner Laurie Nelson Capener showcases a detailed family history book for each surname and simple, elegant design elements for a stunning black and white layout. Machine stitch black, gray and white cardstocks as a color-blocked background. Double mat black-and-white photos; mount with clear photo corners. Print photo captions on white cardstock. Adhere letter stickers around die-cut trees. Mount thin strips of black cardstock as border around photos and title. Sandwich punched fleurs-de-lis from black and white cardstocks and foam spacers; attach snap and mount at border corners. Print charts for cover of book on vellum; layer over tree printed on white cardstock. Mount on black cardstock with clear photo corners. Print family history and mount photos on white cardstock for inside pages; bind with comb spine. Attach back cover of completed chart books over double-matted patterned paper with eyelets.

Laurie Nelson Capener, Providence, Utah: Memory Makers Family Tree Contest Winner

patterned papers (Scrap Ease); die-cut trees (EK Success); letter stickers (Making Memories); presentation binding system (GBC Docubind); fleur-de-lis punch (Anna Griffin); clear photo corners; foam spacers; brads

The New Kid on the Block

BUILD ON A PLAYFUL THEME

A clever play on words and faux building block tower welcomes Kelly's youngest child to the family. Punch photos with 1½" square punch; round corners. Mount photos and letter stickers for title on 2" matted patterned paper squares with rounded corners. Arrange on page as shown; embellish center block with letter tiles. Adhere balance of letter stickers for title. Journal with black pen.

Kelly Peterson, Altoona, Iowa

patterned papers (Amscan, Bazzill); letter stickers (Making Memories); letter tiles (Creative Imaginations); 1½" square punch and corner rounder (Creative Memories)

Family...The Essence of Life

BUILD A BLOCK TOWER FOR UNIQUE FAMILY TIES

Ulla's large, extended family of stepchildren and half-siblings treasure each other as true brothers and sisters, and even the family pets are held in high esteem in her handmade/computer-generated layout. Scan older photos and shoot new ones if needed; edit and size images with image-editing software. Create blocks in a drawing program, such as Adobe Illustrator; import into image-editing software. Layer photos and text onto blocks and print each individual block on glossy photo paper; cut out blocks. Create page title and name borders in the same manner as the blocks; print onto photo paper and cut out. Assemble page, working from the eldest generation across the bottom of page to the youngest generation across the top, and add title and name borders to finish.

Ulla Sessions, Aliso Viejo, California

image-editing software (Adobe InDesign); drawing software (Adobe Illustrator); glossy photo paper

Family Tree

PUNCH A VICTORIAN BORDER

Laurie features a husband and wife during their "autumn years" amidst warm, seasonal colors, dainty leaf buttons and a lovely punched Victorian border. Layer punched oak leaves, flowers and quasar over punched swirls for border design; complete with sliced cardstock strips on matted ivory background paper. Print bow-tie ancestor chart, photos, genealogy information and quote on white cardstock. Single and double mat; mount photos on page with clear photo corners. Mount die-cut title and dimensional tree sticker; embellish tree and page with leaf buttons.

Laurie Nelson Capener, Providence, Utah

patterned papers (Carolee's Creations); die-cut letters (QuicKutz); oak leaf and quasar punches (Family Treasures); swirl and mini, small and large flower punches (Marvy); tree die cut (EK Success); leaf buttons (Jesse James)

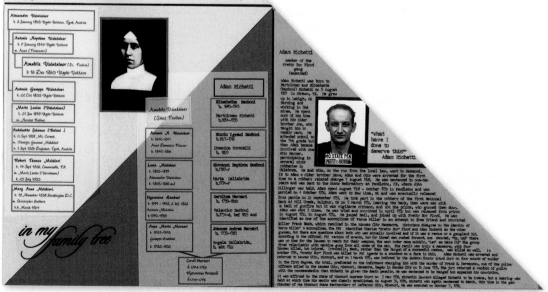

Saints and Sinners

CHRONICLE THE LIVES OF LEGENDARY ANCESTORS

Diagonally cut fold-out flaps conceal accounts about the lives of two colorful characters in Mary Anne's family tree. Mount diagonally cut gold and burgundy cardstocks on black cardstock background. Create fold-out flaps from a second set of diagonally cut cardstock mounted on scored and folded black cardstock "hinge" strips. Horizontally and vertically mount hinges to the back of black cardstock. Mount patterned paper on front of flaps. Hand cut title from gold and burgundy cardstocks. Print genealogy information and ancestral stories on vellum. Mat photos; mount on inside and outside of layout.

Mary Anne Walters, Ramsdell, Hampshire, England; Photos: See page 110

patterned papers (Scrap Ease); cardstock (Bazzill); vellum

Melchiori-Walters Family Tree

BUILD A SYMBOLIC BRIDGE

Mary Anne centers her children in the middle of a circular fan chart that was designed as a symbolic bridge between two families. Mount matted photos on matted patterned paper background. Hand cut title surnames; vertically mount. Print balance of title on transparency; mount at bottom of page. Cut circles in a variety of sizes from solid and patterned papers; layer with cropped photos as shown. Write genealogy information inside and around circles with colored pens.

Mary Anne Walters, Ramsdell, Hampshire, England

patterned paper (Scrap Ease); textured cardstock (Bazzill); transparency

Nichols Family Tree

USE EYELETS AND JUMP RINGS FOR CONNECTION

Helen uses eyelets and jump rings to dangle tiny tags and create family connections between her ancestors. Tear green and brown cardstocks to create tree; mount on background paper. Frame cropped photos with cardstock. Print family history on cardstock; trim into tiny tags and photo captions. Follow the step below to attach eyelets. Mount family history pieces in place by connecting tags and captions with jump rings. Follow the steps below to create shrink art leaves. Complete page with scattered, punched paper and shrink art leaves.

Helen Nichols, Hamilton, Montana

leaf punches (Marvy, Provo Craft); markers (EK Success); earth-tone papers; eyelets and eyelet setting tools; jump rings; shrink plastic; heat-embossing gun

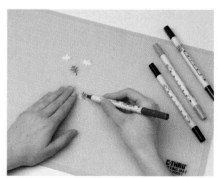

1 To add eyelets, punch a ¼" hole for eyelet. Insert eyelet; flip eyelet and paper over. Place pointed-end of setter into protruding end of eyelet. Tap setter with hammer; remove setter. Tap eyelet top again to complete the set.

1 Punch larger leaves from shrink-art plastic. If desired, brush front and back of each leaf with powder to prevent sticking during shrinkage. One at a time, heat each leaf with a heat gun for a few seconds, holding it down with a craft stick. The leaves will curl during heating and flatten when shrinkage is complete.

2 Use markers to colorize the leaves and add vein details.

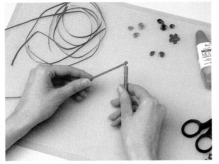

Nylander-Olson Family Tree

CONNECT FAMILY WITH QUILLED PAPER BRANCHES

Debbie used quilling to re-create a quilt design she liked and link two family surnames with colorful branches. Tape two 12 x 12" sheets of cardstock together on back with removable artist's tape. Mount patterned paper and tree die cut at center; use a metal ruler and craft knife to split patterned paper in half along cardstock seam and remove tape. Mark a vertical line 2½" in at left and right sides of cardstocks; score with a bone folder and make the folds for hidden journaling panels. Follow the step at left to create quilled pieces. Punch family names into squares; mount in order with foam spacers over quilling. Complete with journaled vellum panels attached with eyelets.

Debbie Weller, Kalispell, Montana

patterned paper (Colorbök); tree die cut (Sizzix); quilling papers (Quilled Creations); vellum; slotted quilling tool; square punch; foam spacers; eyelets

1 Insert one end of paper strip into tip of slotted needle. Roll handle of tool with one hand to form a circle; secure loose end with liquid adhesive. Gently pinch the coiled circle at one end, coaxing it into a teardrop shape. Repeat until desired teardrops are completed. Adhere to page as desired to form flowers and leaves.

All Our Dreams

ASSEMBLE A MODERN FAMILY TREE

Anything goes when it comes to the look of a family tree. MaryJo's modern layout and use of bright colors reflects her family's unique characteristics and captures the historic value of her immediate family. Layer red and green patterned papers for background. Print family information, lines and text on transparency and clip art tree on white cardstock. Layer transparency over tree; attach eyelets. Mount ribbon along transparency edges; string wire leaves on ribbon. Mount embroidered word labels. Scan, tint, print and silhouette cut family faces.

MaryJo Regier, Memory Makers Books

red patterned paper (Keeping Memories Alive); green patterned paper (source unknown); transparency/clear canvas (Magic Scraps); ribbon (Making Memories); wire leaves (Westrim); embroidered word labels (Me & My Big Ideas); tree clip art; eyelets

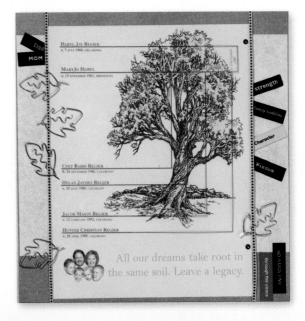

A
Piece
of
My
Family
Tree

United States Department of the Interior

BUREAU OF INDIAN AFFAIRS
Drawer H
Talihina, Oklahoma 74571

JUL 1 7 1977

CERTIFICATE OF DEGREE OF INDIAN BLOOD

This is to certify that according to the records of this office and pursuant
to the provisions of Sec. 2, Act of August 4, 1947 (61 Stat. 732)

CYNTHIA DIANE MC CONNELL   born   2-20-58

is of   1/8   degree   Choctaw   Indian blood.

The lineal ancestors of the above-named are as follows:

NAME   TRIBE   ROLL NO.   DEGREE
Father:
Mother: Juanita Smith   Choctaw   NE   1/4
Paternal Grandfather:
Paternal Grandmother:
Maternal Grandfather:
Maternal Grandmother: Anna Mae Brummett Choctaw   NE   1/2
Mat. Gr. Grandmother: Selin Maytobe   Choctaw   1380   4/4

VERIFICATION:

Certificate of Birth establishes the applicant to be the daughter of
Juanita Smith, a not enrolled Choctaw parent.

Certificate of Degree of Indian Blood issued to Juanita Smith dated May 19,
1976, confirms the above ancestry and degree of Indian blood.

Acting   Superintendent

ANY ALTERATION IN THE ABOVE CERTIFICATE AUTOMATICALLY RENDERS IT NULL AND VOID.

Cynthia Diane
McConnell

Juanita Smith

Anna Mae Brummett

Selin Maytobe

What an interesting history
I have! My Great Grandmother
was a true American. She was a
full blood Choctaw Indian. She,
along with her family was part of
the Indian Removal Act where
she walked on the "Trail of Tears"
from Mississippi to the Indian
Territory before Oklahoma became a
state. She was an original enrollee
on the Dawes Roll, which the United
States government used to document
all the Indians that had been
relocated to the Indian Territory.
As a result of the hardships
she endured, she died when my
Grandmother, Anna Mae
was 2 years old. She must have
endured a lot of pain to leave her
way of life and journey to a new
land and embrace a new way of life!

Cultivating Culture

While tilling your ancestral garden, it is not uncommon to dig up an ethnic background of which you may have been unaware. Perhaps you were 100 percent certain you were of German and Norwegian ancestry, only to discover you also have French Canadian roots! It's easy to celebrate your ethnic heritage in traditional style with scrapbook page elements based on designs and patterns from the culture of your ancestors.

To introduce a country's culture on your family tree pages, immerse yourself in topic-related books at your local public library and browse the Internet. You'll find a plethora of maps, flags, folk art, patterns, clip art, history, heraldry and country symbols and icons to help infuse your family tree pages with rich cultural flavor. Pay attention to traditional colors, specifically in folk art and heraldry, which can add a touch of authenticity.

Whether your ancestors were kilt-clad highlanders from Scotland, Filipino islanders or wealthy Honduran landowners, immerse yourself in the traditions, customs, history and folk art of your ancestral homeland. You will be richly rewarded with family tree scrapbook pages that speak not only to the heart but that cultivate and sow true ethnic pride.

Cynthia McConnell-McNeil, Folkston, Georgia
See page 110.

We Are One From Many

CROSS-STITCH A TREASURED FAMILY HEIRLOOM

Jill's multi-page composition features a cross-stitched treasured heirloom design as well as surname border strips and embellishments for a fold-out presentation of her family's ancestral roots. Create fold-out pages in sections. Piece pages together and mount back to back upon completion. Print subdued photo background on vellum from photos scanned and lightened with image-editing software. Mount on black cardstock using vellum tape. Mat ancestral photos and mount with foam spacers; layer with printed genealogy information and handmade, pre-made and die-cut embellishments. Mount cross-stitched "Tree of Life" on black cardstock quadrants. Represent ancestral countries of origin with a paper-pieced flag border cut from colored cardstocks.

Jill Bulgin, Severna Park, Maryland

black cardstock and multicolored cardstock scraps; cross-stitched cover design (source unknown), family names and hearts; wide array of assorted handmade and pre-made miniature page accents based on family members' interests; handmade country flags

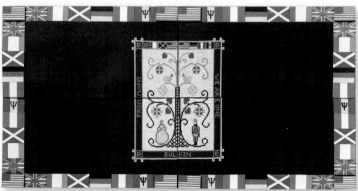

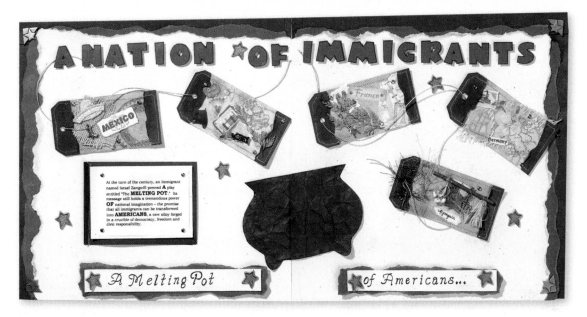

A Nation of Immigrants

REPRESENT NATIVE ROOTS

Sharon and her sister worked together to research their roots and create a layout that not only represent the diverse background of their heritage, but also of the country they call home. Layer torn and chalked ivory and red cardstocks over brown cardstock background; mount decorative metal corners. Cut two sets of tags from tan patterned paper and brown cardstock; add color to tan tags with chalk. Tear top and bottom from brown tag; layer over tan tag and stitch around edges. Collage each tag with torn patterned papers, pressed flowers and leaves, mesh, dimensional and thematic stickers, fibers and charms. Attach brads and punch holes; link tags together on page with jute string. Cut title letters from red cardstock using template; ink edges and mount with foam spacers. Write subtitle on ivory cardstock; layer over torn red cardstock strips and mount with foam spacers. Print family history on vellum and white papers; cut to booklet size. Mat text for cover and attach brads. Sandwich printed pages between brown cardstock covers; vertically stitch to bind. Crumple, flatten and chalk die-cut pot; vertically slice before mounting on pages. Embellish page and title strips with metal stars.

Sharon Thiesen, Bourbonnais, Illinois; Dianna Dominguez, Pearland, Texas

patterned papers (Making Memories, Paperbilities); lettering template (source unknown); metal stars (Making Memories); stickers (Mrs. Grossman's, Tumblebeasts); charms (Charm and Bead Collectibles); brads; jute

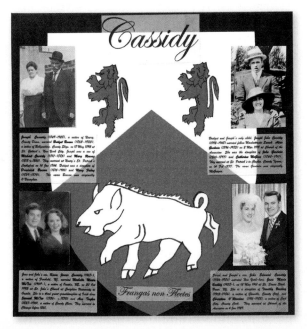

Cassidy

PAPER PIECE A FAMILY CREST

Shelly chronicles her husband's proud Irish heritage atop a time-honored family crest. Piece together family crest from red and white cardstocks; mount on black cardstock background. Print genealogy information, family history and title on vellum.

Shelly Cassidy, Omaha, Nebraska

black, red and white cardstocks; vellum

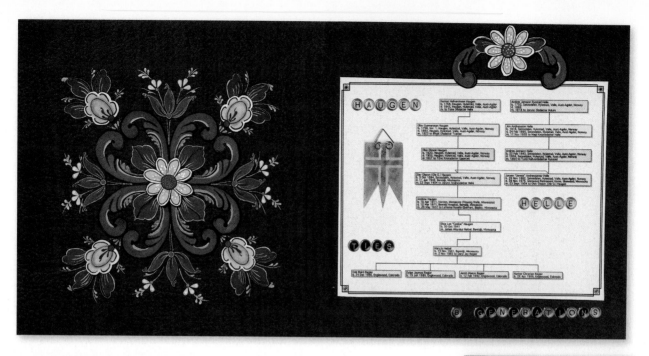

Haugen-Helle Ties

REPLICATE A CULTURAL FOLK ART

MaryJo mimics a traditional Rogaland-style rosemaling painting pattern with paper piecing to highlight her Norwegian ancestry. Try this with any culturally related quilting, painting, stained glass or ethnic pattern for a family tree with homespun appeal. Follow the steps below to create the paper-pieced Norwegian rosemaling art. For right page, adhere computer-printed pedigree chart with eyelets. Rub country's flag with walnut ink; adhere with foam spacer and decorative clip. Finish with paper-pieced accent and letter stickers.

MaryJo Regier, Memory Makers Books

pattern on page 109; dark blue cardstock; scraps of slate blue, light blue, dark green, dark rust, mustard and gray cardstocks; mini teardrop, ¼", ¹⁄₁₆" punches (optional); metallic blue, gold, yellow and white gel pens (Staedtler); metallic blue, black and white Galaxy markers (American Crafts); black journaling pen; vintage chalk colors (Craf-T); Reunion 8.0 pedigree chart (Leister Productions); country flag clip art; letter stickers (K & Company); decorative clip (Making Memories); foam spacers; permanent tape adhesive; eyelets

MaryJo's paper-pieced art is based on the actual painting of Joanne MacVey, a Vesterheim Gold Medalist Rosemaler from Blue Grass, Iowa, and author of the new book, Rosemaling Heirlooms of Tomorrow.

1 Photocopy pattern, scaling to desired size. Cut out pattern pieces. You only need to use one-quarter of the pattern and the flower in the center and simply duplicate the cut pieces three more times to reproduce the art versus cutting out the entire pattern.

2 Place pattern pieces onto appropriate-colored cardstock scraps and trace around each pattern as many times as needed using picture of art above as a guideline. Cut out cardstock pieces. Punch tiny teardrops and circles from cardstock scraps.

3 Using art shown above as a guideline, add detail to cardstock pieces with chalks and complementary-colored Galaxy, gel and journaling markers and pens. Chalk pieces for depth. Add chalk last to mute pen details and to preserve pen tips from chalk bleeds.

4 Begin assembly, starting at the center of cardstock background, building the art outwards and spacing cardstock pieces evenly as you go. Mount floral center with foam spacers for dimension. Complete with hand-drawn leaf and scroll details directly on background.

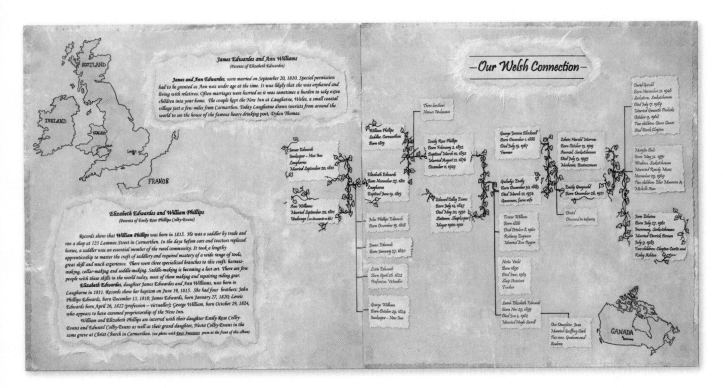

Our Welsh Connection

TRACE VINES AND ANCESTRAL HOMELAND MAPS

Jane's beautifully simplistic, information-packed page spread features drawings of her ancestors' countries and delicate vines to connect family members. Print title and journaling onto parchment, tear and chalk edges, mat with torn mulberry. Print family names and dates onto parchment; trim into shapes with deckle scissors; mount in proper order on page spread. Follow the step below for tracing map outlines and vines onto vellum. Assemble all page components and mount on patterned background paper.

Jane Brown, Rocky Mountain House, Alberta, Canada

pattern on page 109; patterned paper (Karen Foster Design); vellum, parchment and mulberry papers; map of ancestral country; deckle scissors; chalk; black journaling pen

1 Copy map to desired size. Layer vellum over map in position desired; tape to light box or a sunny window with removable artist's tape. Use black journaling pen to trace country outline. Photocopy the vine pattern on page 109 and repeat this step, tracing vines as desired to link family members.

Filipino Roots

CULTIVATE CULTURAL FAMILY TREE

Janetta honors her family's Filipino culture with ornamental rows of bamboo shoots and a woven background made from the plant that is so familiar to her native country. Slice frame from green cardstock; mount over textured bamboo paper for border and ink around edges. Assemble family tree branches from inked bamboo embellishments; layer with punched bamboo shoots as descendant lines. Layer genealogy information printed on mulberry paper. Mount die-cut title and silhouette-cut photo images; secure bamboo clips at page corners.

Janetta Abucejo Wieneke, Memory Makers Books

bamboo paper (Global Solutions); die-cut letters (QuicKutz); bamboo embellishments (EK Success); bamboo shoot punch (All Night Media); bamboo clips (7 Gypsies); mulberry paper (Pulsar); brown and moss green ink (Clearsnap)

Kaeo Family

PAPER PIECE HAWAIIAN PARADISE

Becki's paper-pieced palm tree bears the family name that inspired her to find her husband's roots amongst the beauty of the Hawaiian islands. Becki places her family within a colorful Hawaiian scene. Mount torn green cardstock mountain across both patterned paper background pages. Freehand cut and assemble palm tree from green patterned paper, brown foam paper and tan textured cardstock. Mount die-cut paper doll and kayak. Adhere tiny gold and clear glass pebbles under palm tree with double-stick tape. Print photo captions on vellum. Mount cropped photos and photo captions on palm leaves. Layer family information over remaining photos matted on lavender cardstock; attach eyelets. Assemble title words from a variety of elements: adhere letter stickers on coconuts, bend and twist wire into word, and string letter beads on photo mat. Complete page with quilled sun and layered punched flowers.

Becki Mays, Huntsville, Alabama

patterned papers (source unknown); textured paper (Emagination Crafts); foam paper; wire; letter stickers (Provo Craft); tiny glass marbles (Halcraft); paper doll (EK Success); letter beads (Westrim); decorative cross punch (All Night Media); flower die cuts (source unknown); eyelets

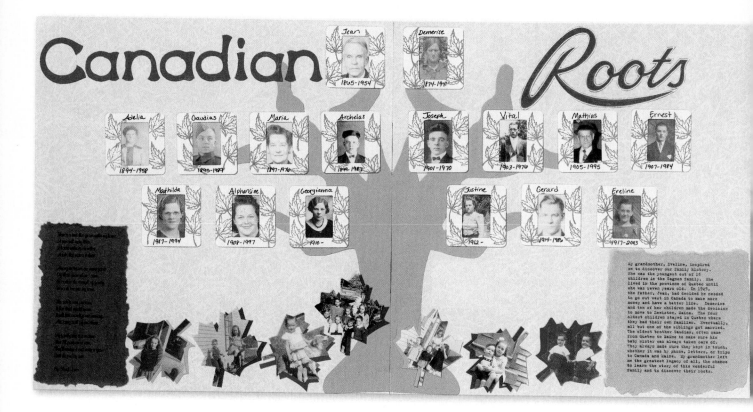

Canadian Roots

STAMP SLIDE MOUNT FRAMES

Suzanne's use of cropped and stamped maple leaves represents the fact that each of her ancestors adds to the fullness of her Canadian family tree. Cropped photo leaves and stamped slide mount frames represent Suzanne's Canadian roots. Cut tree and maple leaves from colored cardstocks and photos using template; mount tree on patterned paper background. Layer photo and cardstock leaves; scatter along bottom of page. Stamp leaves on slide mount frames; mount over photos. Write names and dates on frames. Mount die-cut letters for first title word; handcut second title word. Print poem and journaling on cardstock; tear edges.

Suzanne Warner, Auburn, Maine

patterned paper (EK Success); lettering template (Provo Craft); slide mount frames (Design Originals); maple leaf stamp (source unknown); tree and maple leaf template (source unknown)

The Munoz-Meers Family Times

MAKE HEADLINES WITH ANCESTRAL STORIES

Extra! Extra! Read all about Goldie's ancestors whose stories of survival and achievement sound like they are taken right from the pages of a history book. Print ancestral "newspaper" and genealogy information on yellow patterned paper; mount on black scrapbook page. Adhere gold sticker strips along side and bottom of newspaper. Crop genealogy information into ovals; mat and embellish with sticker. Adhere sticker border.

Goldie and Melanie Meers, Westminster, Colorado

patterned paper (All My Memories); stickers (Creative Memories, Mrs. Grossman's)

Distinctly Kiwi in the USA

UNITE CULTURAL AND FAMILY HISTORY

Jan creates an educational game of hide-and-seek with layered fold-out flaps and tags that explain her family's New Zealand Maori culture and ancestral history. Start by making the following items: Score and fold all vertical and horizontal fold-out flaps from blue cardstock. Create large fold-out flaps by scoring and folding cardstock 1" from one edge; align and adhere 1" flap to back of cardstock background. Cut continent shapes from blue and green cardstocks. Cross-stitch words. Cut large title letters from green cardstock using template. Silhouette cut cultural characters from patterned papers. Cut tags for each family member from blue (maternal line) and green (paternal line) cardstocks using template. Print ancestral information, cultural terms, geographic locations, song lyrics and quotes on green cardstock and patterned vellum. Begin assembly with the left page. Layer continent shapes with matted photo adorned with decorative corners and bird image on matted patterned paper background. Add dimension to character with foam spacers. Assemble title on fold-out flap from stitched words and metal letter charms attached to blue cardstock strip with brads. Complete title at bottom of page with letter stickers and cardstock letters embellished with star brads. Open fold-out panel; mount cross-stitched words and letters on bottom panel and matted photo on top panel. Adhere silver letter stickers and tiles on blue cardstock strips; mount with brads over matted photos. On left side, layer small vertical fold-out flap on large fold-out flap. Assemble stitched words and cardstock letters on outside of small fold-out. Inside, adhere silver letter stickers and tiles on blue cardstock strips; mount with brads over matted photos. Layer character, song lyrics printed on patterned vellum and continent shapes on right fold-out flap; attach star brads. Mount stitched words and buttons. Open large flaps; mount patterned paper, continent shapes and geographical locations as shown. Mat printed vellum sayings and cultural terms on blue cardstock; attach star brads. Assemble metal letter stickers and cardstock letters at top of page. Mount ancestral information with photos on cardstock tags; group together family members and mount with star brads as shown. Mount double-matted photo embellished with star brad and metal decorative corners.

Jan Brook, Littleton, Colorado

patterned papers (Bright Eyes, Karen Foster Design); letter stickers (EK Success); metal letter stickers (All My Memories); star brads (Making Memories); metal photo corners (Boutique Trims); lettering template (C-Thru Ruler); vellum

Patton Family Tree

COMMEMORATE STORIES OF SURVIVAL

Sue cultivates a beautiful setting to memorialize her ancestors who have stepped through heaven's gate after surviving attacks in the Revolutionary War, imprisonment in Glasgow and years of famine and disease. Print Irish blessing and journaling on patterned vellum; mount patterned vellum and paper on burgundy cardstock for background. Print genealogy information on same patterned paper as background; cut to size and mat. Silhouette cut large shamrock clip art; layer with handcut title. Mat two photos and mount photo captions on blue vellum shaded with chalks. Scatter punched shamrocks on page.

Sue Little, Poplar Bluff, Missouri

patterned paper and vellum (Paper Adventures); shamrock punch (source unknown); chalks

The Journey

TUCK FAMILY INFORMATION INTO MINI POCKETS

Renee describes her journey to motherhood alongside the family structure that is tucked tidily into little pockets labeled with ancestors' names. Layer torn and inked cardstock and printed transparency on blue cardstock background. Slice around large letter on printed transparency with a craft knife; slide edge of postcard under sliced area. Layer printed transparency strip over photos mounted on torn border; attach small brads. Print journaling and quote on gray cardstock; color with chalk. Mount journaling on torn and chalked cardstock. Tear edges around quote; mount both with small brads. Create envelopes from blue cardstock using template; stamp family name and ink edges. Print genealogy information on blue cardstock; cut into small tags and emboss edges. Attach eyelet and tie with fibers before sliding into corresponding envelope. Mount decorative metal plaque. Slide fibers through square concho; attach to page.

Renee Fink, Palisade, Nebraska

printed transparency (Creative Imaginations); brads; envelope template (ScrapGoods); letter stamps (Purple Onion Designs); eyelets; fibers; metal plaque (Making Memories)

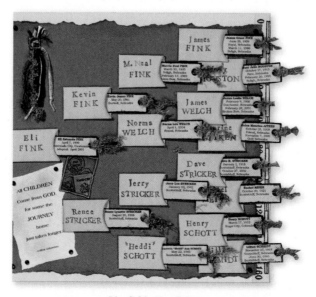

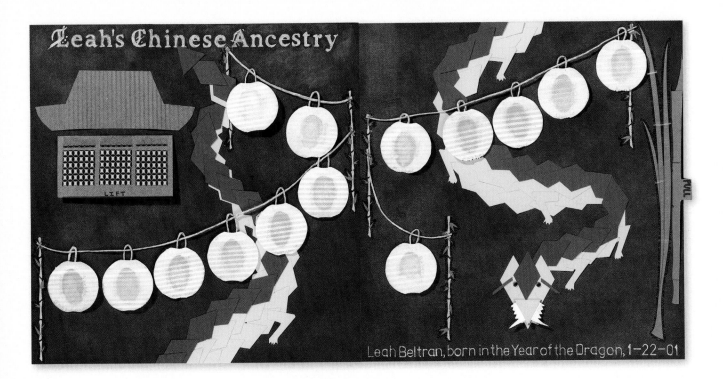

Leah's Chinese Ancestry

HANG GENERATIONAL LANTERNS

Laura illuminates the faces of family members on hanging paper lanterns that dangle over cultural Chinese icons. Write title across black cardstock background with metallic gold and silver pens using template; add color to background with colored chalks. Piece together dragon's body from diamonds punched from green cardstocks, rhinestone eyes and freehand-cut legs and teeth. Sandwich teeth in between folded green and red diamond mouth. Cut pagoda roof from brown crimped cardstock. Make pagoda base from fold-out journaling flap; adhere stickers and journaling. Mount tops of crimped vellum circles over photos mounted on yellow patterned paper circles for lanterns. Secure hemp string handles on back of layered lanterns. String lanterns on hemp; secure ends of hemp string under sliced sections of bamboo sticker. Adhere marsh reed sticker. Create a hidden descendant chart; draw chart on green cardstock before cutting into slide-out element with pull tab and extended arms.

Laura Tate Beltran, Arundel, Maine

patterned papers (source unknown); Asian-themed stickers (Current); chalk; circle and oval templates; vellum; diamond punch; beads; paper crimper; hemp string; letter templates

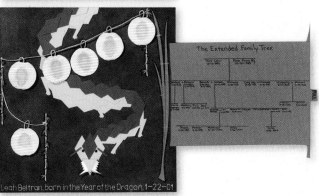

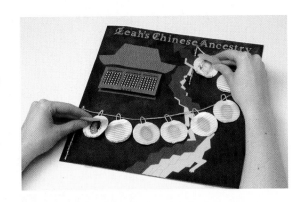

One common cord that ties the Walker family together is their love for the outdoors in particular, fishing. It is well known that this has been a long time family tradition passed down through the generations. Jonathan tells many stories of going out to Fish Lake in Utah with his family. His Grandfather even helped create the road that leads down to the lake. Many camping trips

The Walker Family
Passing down traditions

"In the end it's not what you catch that counts, it's the memory you bring home and the bonds of friendship created that will last forever."

The Walker Family

Growing a Hybrid

There are many genealogical facts that just don't lend themselves well to a traditional family tree, a pedigree chart or a cultural ancestry scrapbook page. That's what we call a hybrid. During your family history research, you're bound to come across those distinctive family traits that stand out as something truly unique.

Perhaps your ancestral photo collection includes the beloved ships of a great-great uncle or generations of women photographed in the same heirloom dress. Or maybe you've uncovered a patronymic naming pattern that has been carried on throughout the decades or generations of wild hairstyles. Here's another hybrid possibility: You've simply come to the conclusion that your family tree really is full of nuts!

Some scrapbookers who come across interesting, often comical, tidbits while researching their ancestry create a historical family presentation that is neither a family tree nor a pedigree chart—it's an innovative and cleverly designed hybrid.

When shaking your family tree, spend a day in yesteryear and set aside those out-of-the-ordinary ancestral finds to help you grow a hybrid page. Nothing's off limits with hybrids; after all, everything's relative! When you've come to your senses, you'll realize that those refreshingly interesting morsels are what really make your family history anything but commonplace!

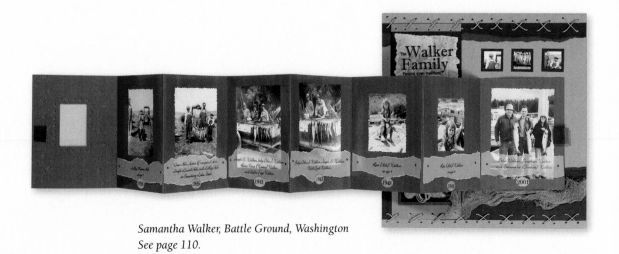

Samantha Walker, Battle Ground, Washington
See page 110.

The Hauss Line

CHART IMMIGRANT TRAVELS

Jenny fashions atop a vintage map a visual record of her ancestors' transatlantic journey and immigration to the United States. Layer patterned papers over teal cardstock background as shown; attach small brads. Secure fiber "travel line" across map with square brads. Magnify ancestors' photos and map detail with pebble stones. Print names and title on vellum. Cut names into tiny jewelry tags; attach with brads. Layer title on walnut-stained tag; tie to fiber line with hemp string. Assemble embellished slide mounts: cover three slide mounts with embossed and patterned papers. Frame two slides with silver and blue aluminum foils. Stamp words and mount over photos; embellish with foreign coin and candlestick. Wrap third slide with fibers and beaded wire; attach stained metal-rimmed tag embellished with dimensional star sticker. Mount one slide mount over torn handmade paper. Mount another over torn and burnt (or inked) map layered over mesh on teal cardstock; adhere map pebble and metallic fiber. Adhere two pieces of folded white cardstock atop another to create fold-out card. Mount journaling, reproduced maps, ancestral information and photos inside panels. Cover front with patterned paper; mount Star of David necklace and layer embellished slide mount over mesh. Mount on blue sanded aluminum. Cover wearable scrapbook with patterned paper. Print journaling, photos and lineage chart on ivory paper; stain with walnut ink before mounting on scrapbook pages. Attach jewelry closure with jump rings so scrapbook can be removed. Fasten on distressed foil-covered tag embellished with handmade paper, painted dimensional boat sticker, mezuzah (container for biblical passages) and fibers.

Jenny Moore Lowe, Lafayette, Colorado

patterned papers (7 Gypsies, Creative Imaginations, Design Originals); mesh paper (Magenta); mini wearable scrapbook (Creative Imaginations); letter stamps (Hero Arts); square brads (Creative Impressions); map pebbles (Magic Scraps); decorating foils (AMACO); dimensional stickers (EK Success); slide mounts; metal-rimmed tags; fibers; walnut ink; brads; clear pebbles; handmade paper; vintage coin; candlestick; mezuzah; Star of David necklace

The Descendants of Adams Dodd

DOCUMENT THE LOVES OF A MARINER'S LIFE

Vickie's eye-catching color palette, handmade sails and canvas-printed ships shore up her tribute to a great-great uncle mariner and won her first prize in the Memory Makers Family Tree contest. Double mat patterned paper background on teal and brown cardstocks. Print photos on canvas photo paper; double and triple mat on coordinating cardstocks. Print title, genealogy information, journaling and quote on patterned papers and vellum. Double mat title block; layer over torn brown cardstock. Adhere decorative sticker and gold frames around title words and genealogy information. Mount gold embroidery thread for ancestral lines. Double mat journaling; embellish with knotted twine. Cover chipboard with patterned paper for booklet covers. Embellish front cover with letter stickers, vellum and nautical charm; attach hinges. Bind journaling pages along top with clear tape; mount to inside back cover. Stitch along edges of canvas "sails"; attach eyelets and lace with twine. Mat quote; embellish with knotted twine and nautical charm. Mount balance of nautical-themed charms.

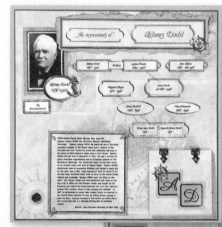

Vickie Dodd-Edgerton, Rochester, Minnesota; Memory Makers Family Tree Contest Winner

patterned papers (Creative Imaginations, SEI); canvas photo paper (Avery); decorative frames (Nunn Design); sticker frames (Stampendous); letter stickers (Elegant Scrapbooks); nautical charms (American Tag); canvas; eyelets; gold embroidery thread; hinges; chipboard; vellum; twine

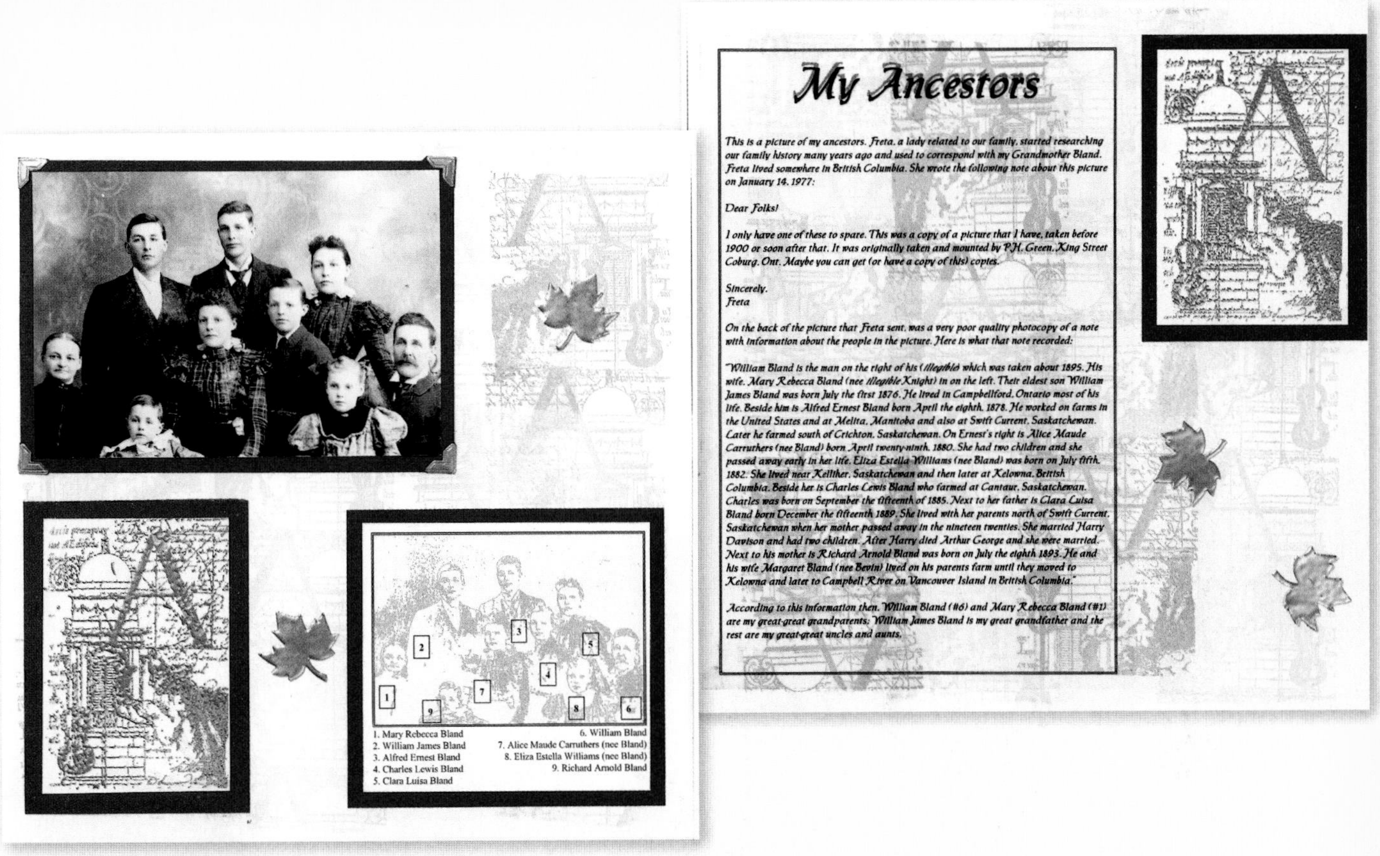
My Ancestors
This is a picture of my ancestors. Freta, a lady related to our family, started researching our family history many years ago and used to correspond with my Grandmother Bland. Freta lived somewhere in British Columbia. She wrote the following note about this picture on January 14, 1977:
Dear Folks!
I only have one of these to spare. This was a copy of a picture that I have, taken before 1900 or soon after that. It was originally taken and mounted by P.H. Green, King Street Coburg, Ont. Maybe you can get (or have a copy of this) copies.
Sincerely,
Freta
On the back of the picture that Freta sent, was a very poor quality photocopy of a note with information about the people in the picture. Here is what that note recorded:
"William Bland is the man on the right of his (illegible) which was taken about 1895. His wife, Mary Rebecca Bland (nee illegible Knight) in on the left. Their eldest son William James Bland was born July the first 1876. He lived in Campbellford, Ontario most of his life. Beside him is Alfred Ernest Bland born April the eighth, 1878. He worked on farms in the United States and at Melita, Manitoba and also at Swift Current, Saskatchewan. Later he farmed south of Crichton, Saskatchewan. On Ernest's right is Alice Maude Carruthers (nee Bland) born April twenty-ninth, 1880. She had two children and she passed away early in her life. Eliza Estella Williams (nee Bland) was born on July fifth, 1882. She lived near Kellther, Saskatchewan and then later at Kelowna, British Columbia. Beside her is Charles Lewis Bland who farmed at Cantaur, Saskatchewan. Charles was born on September the fifteenth of 1885. Next to her father is Clara Luisa Bland born December the fifteenth 1889. She lived with her parents north of Swift Current, Saskatchewan when her mother passed away in the nineteen twenties. She married Harry Davison and had two children. After Harry died Arthur George and she were married. Next to his mother is Richard Arnold Bland was born on July the eighth 1893. He and his wife Margaret Bland (nee Bevin) lived on his parents farm until they moved to Kelowna and later to Campbell River on Vancouver Island in British Columbia."
According to this information then, William Bland (#6) and Mary Rebecca Bland (#1) are my great-great grandparents; William James Bland is my great grandfather and the rest are my great-great uncles and aunts.
1
2
3
4
5
6
7
8
9
1. Mary Rebecca Bland
2. William James Bland
3. Alfred Ernest Bland
4. Charles Lewis Bland
5. Clara Luisa Bland
6. William Bland
7. Alice Maude Carruthers (nee Bland)
8. Eliza Estella Williams (nee Bland)
9. Richard Arnold Bland

My Ancestors

STAMP UNIQUE IMAGERY TO SHOWCASE DATA

Steven transforms simple white cardstock and one photo into stunning imagery with one stamp and his photo software. Follow the step below to create custom background paper. Stamp and emboss two additional images and mat with paper for page accents. Punch maple leaves from cardstock, ink and emboss with gold embossing powder. Scan photo. Use software to trace outlines of people, assign numbers and type a numeric/name list for identification; print on cardstock and mat. You can also trace outlines of people onto cardstock or vellum by using a light box or sunny window and a black journaling pen. Print ancestral information on vellum. Assemble all elements and mount across pages.

Steven Bland, Oshawa, Ontario, Canada

white and navy cardstocks; white vellum; background stamp (Inkadinkado); multicolor metallic pigment ink pad (Tsukineko); gold photo corners (Canson); brayer; image-editing software; maple leaf punch; gold embossing powder

1 To achieve an even and variegated stamped-image background, roll brayer across multicolor ink pad and then roll the inked brayer across the stamp. Stamp paper in vertical rows, re-inking only as needed to achieve the variegated look. Repeat process as needed until background paper is covered with stamped imagery.

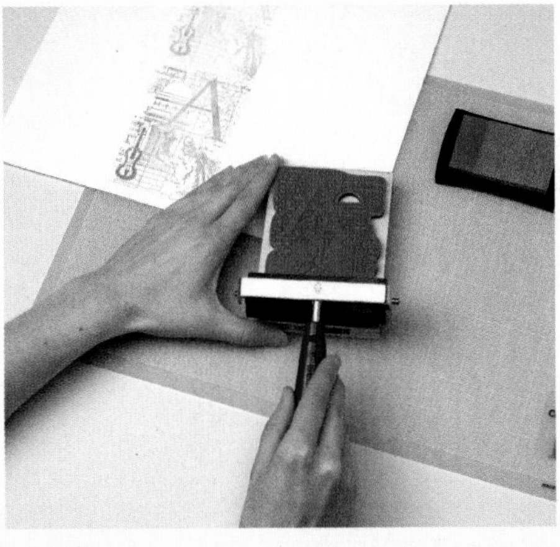

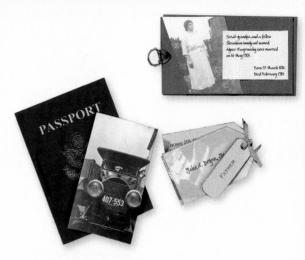

Traveling Down the Road of Life

SHOW LINEAGE WITH TAG CLUSTERS

The travels taken by Suzanne's ancestors form the road map of her family tree today. Diagonally mount torn patterned paper on rust cardstock background. Print titles, journaling, genealogy information and photo captions on vellum, ivory and tan cardstocks. Ink edges of title blocks; mat on torn blue cardstock and attach eyelets. Freehand fold and cut notched photo pockets from colored cardstocks; mount photos with metallic photo corners. Create pullout information cards with photos and captions mounted on colored cardstocks; attach doorknocker charm at edge of each and slide inside pocket. Assemble genealogy tag clusters; cut information into various shaped tags. Layer printed vellum over tags collaged with torn solid and patterned papers. Attach eyelets to all tags; tie together with fibers. Re-create passport with real scanned and printed passport cover. Chalk edges of printed journaling pages; punch holes and bind with cover using leather string. Store passport inside envelope made from patterned vellum and template; mount second title block. Mount compass embellishment.

Suzanne Drgon, Virginia Beach, Virginia

patterned papers (Club Scrap, PSX Design); patterned vellum (Club Scrap); doorknocker charms (Foofala); envelope template (C-Thru Ruler); compass (Magic Scraps); eyelets; leather; fibers; photo corners

Some Have a Nut in the Family

FEATURE FAMILY FUN

Erica's parents have always encouraged living a "fun" life, so it's no surprise that she refers to her family with such humor. Mount vertically sliced die-cut tree on both pages with foam spacers. Print title and genealogy information on white cardstock; mat on brown cardstock. Mat photos and printed text on brown cardstock. Write names on premade acorn die-cuts. Pierce holes and tie brown embroidery thread loops; dangle from tree branches.

Erica Goulding, Arlington, Texas

patterned paper (Frances Meyer); die-cut tree (Deluxe Designs); premade die cuts (My Mind's Eye); embroidery floss

3 Generations

STENCIL AND DRY EMBOSS COORDINATED ELEMENTS

Colleen uses a single brass stencil to create custom-coordinated background paper and tags for a unified look. Follow the steps below to make stencil background and tags. Assemble page elements and mount permanently in place. Add printed title and journaling to finish page.

Colleen Rundgren for American Traditional Designs, Northwood, New Hampshire

sage, rust and cream cardstocks; vellum; tree stencil, stencil paints, stencil brush and palette (American Traditional Designs); embossing stylus; brads

1 Hold tree stencil on cardstock in desired position. Working with one paint color at a time, dip brush into paint. Swirl brush briskly onto a paper towel to remove excess paint. Tap or rub brush through stencil. Repeat process in second colors, applying stenciling randomly until page is covered.

2 To dry emboss stencil, place stencil behind tag and secure with removable artist's tape. Place face up on light box and trace around image on stencil to emboss image onto tag.

3 Remove stencil and tape, turn over and place stencil on top of embossed image; hold stencil in place on tag with removable artist's tape. Rub tag with paint through stencil to add color and dimension.

Time Stand Still

TRY EMULSION LIFT TRANSFERS FOR TIMELESS BEAUTY

Elizabeth combines the use of clever pockets and image transfers to document her heritage on this interactive scrap-book page. Stamp lettering across background page and add ink splotches using stippling brush for aged look. Photocopy and size pocket pattern on page 109 onto white cardstock; cut out pockets. Stamp lettering and images onto pockets in various ink colors, score on fold lines and make pocket folds; mount on page. Cut photo/journaling panels; score and make folds. Expose and process a sheet of film by taking a picture of each heritage picture you want included on the page; let dry 8 to 24 hours. Fill one tray with 160 degrees Fahrenheit water; fill another tray with cold water. Moisten watercolor paper with room-temperature tap water for several seconds; place paper on glass and "laminate" it to the surface with a squeegee. Then follow steps below to create image emulsion transfers. Print title and photo captions, tear edges, age with stippling brush in many colors, chalk title edges and mount. Attach knotted leather pull-tabs to back of photo/journaling panels; insert into pockets.

Elizabeth Kuntz, Richmond, Texas

pattern on page 109; dark orange and cream cardstocks; ; complementary-colored ink pads; stippling brush; thinking of you and Victorian tapestry stamps (Close To My Heart); manuscript background stamp (Hero Arts); pocket watch stamp (Inkadinkado); 59 color instant sheet film and image emulsion transfer kit (both Polaroid Corp.); watercolor paper (Strathmore); leather ribbon. You must have a camera that will shoot Polaroid's 669, 59, 559 or 809 sheet film for this project; see their Web site for more information.

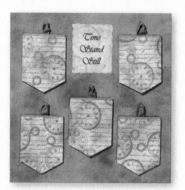

1 Immerse print face-up in hot-water tray for about four minutes. Use tongs to re-move print from hot water and place it in the tray of cold water.

2 Lightly push the emulsion from the edges of the print toward the center. Lift the emul-sion carefully and slowly peel it away from the paper substrate, leaving the emulsion floating in the water. Discard paper substrate.

3 Slip a piece of wax paper under the floating image; grab image at corners and place it onto wax paper. Remove paper from water, flip it over and put back in water to make the image read correctly after it's transferred. Remove wax paper from emulsion and slip it back underneath the floating emulsion. Lift paper in and out of water several times to stretch image and remove wrinkles.

4 When you're satisfied with it, remove the image from the water and place it on the watercolor paper, making sure your wax paper is on top. Rub image with your fingers and carefully remove the wax paper. Straighten and smooth as de-sired. Roll the image with a soft rubber brayer from the middle outward. Hang to dry when finished.

Memories of Home

CREATE A UNIQUE SPECIALTY ALBUM

Kate was inspired to assemble an antique billfold which holds creatively designed ancestral elements after realizing her own wallet was a gathering place of personal memories. Create pattern piece for each wallet section from cardstock; cover with light or dark brown leather specialty papers. Machine-stitch around edges of each pattern piece. For outside front panel, print family tree drawing on transparency; adhere quote sticker. Secure metal letter tags with flat eyelets. Cut wallet clasps from metallic silver paper. For inside left panel, create "personal checks" with ancestral information; print on parchment paper. Photocopy maps of family members' birthplaces; embellish with photos and ancestral details. Tie photocopied letters, photos and miscellaneous ephemera with twine. Embellish premade tag with jewelry scraps and stitched button; mount on front of pocket stitched to inside panel. For inside middle section, stitch plastic shirt tab on cardstock for key chain holder. Attach key ring with keys, dog tag, chain and acrylic hearts. Stitch strip for pen-holder. Make cardholders from layers of sheet protectors. Horizontally stitch leather paper strips at top of each sheet protector; layer over another starting from the top and vertically stitch together. Slice window in leather paper; mount over sheet protector. Print family tree on parchment; slip behind window. Laminate custom-made family I.D. cards and miscellaneous memorabilia; slide into cardholders. For inside right panel, stitch pocket for photo sleeve. Make photo sleeves from acrylic sheet divider. Stitch one edge of stair-stepped laminated photos to one side of divider; crop and tuck other side of divider into pocket. For back panel, overlap brown leather paper sewn to cardstock. Scan photos and print funny money onto green paper; print family history on back.

Kate Featherstone, Dallas, Texas

leather specialty papers (source unknown); assorted "found" metal tags, clasps, jewelry scraps, keys, key ring; twine; buttons; page protectors or transparency; sewing machine or needle and thread; pre-made tag (EK Success); fibers

Their Marks in Time

SHELTER HISTORY BEHIND DECORATIVE PANELS

Tracy, the grand-prize winner of the Memory Makers Family Tree Contest, illustrates the historical saga of her ancestors with an interesting collection of collaged time-period embellishments. Staple muslin fabric to patterned paper background; layer with large clock face, antique watch and watch parts as shown. Adhere letter stickers on wood scrap for title. Wrap with wire; hang sentiment charms from wire. Assemble panels from textured and colored cardstocks. Print journaling and ancestral timeline on vellum; layer with cropped photos inside panels. Attach small hinges to panels and pages with brads. Collage patterned papers, muslin, mesh, feathers, glass bottle, watch parts, buttons, swirl clips, mica tiles, nailheads, stamped wax seal, ink-stained tag, stamped images, embossed metal word, and various time-period charms on front and insides of panels. Heat emboss bookplates with rust embossing powder; stamp dates and mount with brads.

Tracy Liekhus, Erie, Colorado; Memory Makers Family Tree Contest Winner

muslin fabric, patterned paper (Karen Foster Design); metal word (Making Memories); vellum; assorted "found" watch and watch parts, charms, hinges, wood scraps, brads, wire, nailheads, wax seal, glass bottle, mesh, feathers, buttons, clips, mica, bookplates; letter stickers (Rusty Pickle); stamps (source unknown); ink

Unlocking Family Secrets

KEEP FAMILY SECRETS BEHIND CLOSED DOORS

Torrey's collaged and hinged doors open to reveal an archive of color-coded envelopes that hold treasured stories about each relative from the past four generations—which garnered her second prize in the Memory Makers Family Tree contest. Begin by assembling each panel separately. Cover one side of heavy cardboard with black cardstock and other side with burgundy cardstock; diagonally slice and set aside. Cover inside center foam core panel with ivory cardstock; slice window frame and set aside. Piece together black cardstock cover panels; collage with patterned papers, ephemera, letter stickers, clip art, torn and inked papers, framed word bubbles, wax imprint and dimensional embellishments that are relevant to ancestral history. Make sure to slice images or elements that will span two pages before mounting. Add extra dimension to elements by mounting with foam spacers. Turn cover panels over; collage burgundy cardstock with photos, images, ephemera and letter stickers. Adhere gold photo corner stickers on photos. Affix pen sticker to thin strip of foam core before mounting. Collage frame with patterned papers, ephemera, letter and number stickers and postage memorabilia; slice off overhanging images along frame lines. Stamp generational categories on green patterned paper strips; attach on burgundy cardstock with brads. Mount behind collaged foam core frame. Print color-coded categories, family member names and stories on colored and speckled cardstocks. Mount gold-embossed bookplate stickers over color code text at top of frame. Designate one envelope for each family member on both sides of family; color code envelopes according to maternal and paternal lines with green and brown inks. Mount family member names on envelopes; tuck printed story inside. Assemble panel doors with hinges; mount one side of hinge on outside of cover panels and inside of center panel with regular and heart brads. Close doors and mount clasp on cover; slip lock into clasp.

Torrey Miller, Thornton, Colorado; 2003 Memory Makers Master; Memory Makers Family Tree Contest Winner

patterned papers (Anna Griffin, Design Originals, DMD); letter stamps (Rubber Stampede); letter sticker tags (Sticker Studio); typewriter letter stickers (K & Company); monogram stamp (Hallmark); nameplate die cut (QuicKutz); pebble phrases and oval frames (Li'l Davis Designs); premade ephemera (Me & My Big Ideas); woman's face stamp (Stampland); themed stickers and photo corners (EK Success); memorabilia keeper (3L); sealing wax; lace heart; hinges; brads; clasp; gold embossing powder; cardboard; foam core; transparency; heart brads; key charms

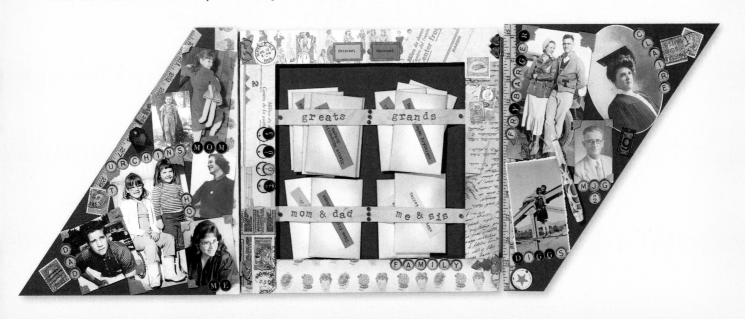

Old Treasures Re-Cherished

BRIDGE THE PAST WITH THE PRESENT

A stamped antique trunk full of fabric, lace and satin ribbon scraps symbolizes the sentimental and historic value of Peggy's treasured family heirlooms. Layer a torn patterned and textured paper border at top of green patterned paper background. Print title on vellum; silhouette cut and color with pink felt-tip pen. Stamp trunk design on ivory cardstock; draw and color floral design. Coat with crystal lacquer; let dry. Fill with lace, ribbon, pearl trim and gold thread. Mount trunk with foam spacers over torn layers of lace and patterned and textured papers. Print journaling on white cardstock; punch corners with decorative corner punch. Outline punched design and edges with gold pen; vertically fold in half. Layer gold decorative frame over green patterned paper; mount metal word charm. Double mat large photo on torn patterned and textured papers; mount on front of folded journaling. Print poem, photo captions and genealogy information on patterned paper. Tear edges and mat on torn textured paper; embellish poem with antique button and tassel. Scan photos; re-size with image-editing

software. Print and mount behind gold oval frames. Cut tags from textured paper using template; outline with gold pen. Embellish with gold decorative corners, fabric, lace, satin ribbon, pearls and buttons. Mount gold decorative frame over center photo caption.

Peggy Adair, Fort Smith, Arkansas; Photo: Oftedahl Photography, Rogers, Arkansas

patterned paper (Daisy D's); textured paper (Provo Craft); trunk stamp (Great Impressions); crystal lacquer (Sakura Hobby Craft); pearl trim (Magic Scraps); gold thread (DMC); decorative corner punch (Family Treasures); gold decorative frames and corners (Nunn Design); tassel (Card Connection); buttons; gold gel pen

One Tree, Many Leaves

STITCH AND FOLD ANCESTRAL POCKETS

Embellished envelopes and stitched pockets become lovely niches for storing ancestral information, photos and memorabilia. Stitch torn green patterned paper strips on pink patterned paper background. Mat photos on brown, bronze and walnut-stained cardstocks; set aside. Cut large tags from patterned papers using template; stitch around edges and attach eyelet over punched square. Mat large photos on bronze cardstock; mount printed captions with eyelets and layer with skeleton leaves as shown. Assemble title from metal letters and words printed on torn walnut-stained cardstock. Print ancestral names on walnut-stained cardstock before cutting, tearing, or folding into desired shape. Store generational photos and memorabilia inside an assortment of stitched and folded pockets. Fold envelope pockets from patterned

papers using template. Stitch torn vellum and patterned paper pockets along two or three edges. Embellish pockets with metal letters, tiny eyelets, buttons, skeleton leaves, walnut-stained tags and satin ribbon. Layer walnut-stained cardstock booklet cover with tan and green patterned papers; stitch along edges of green patterned paper. Print title on ink-stained cardstock; cut into tag, tear edge and attach with eyelet. Bind handwritten ancestral information on walnut-stained pages to cover by stitching down the center of the book. Fashion tie closure with tiny eyelet, punched circle and embroidery thread as shown.

Cori Dahmen, Portland, Oregon; Photos: Decker's Studio

patterned papers (7 Gypsies, Anna Griffin, Club Scrap, Creative Imaginations, Paper Loft, Penny Black, Rusty Pickle); tiny eyelets and metal letters (Making Memories); skeleton leaves (Club Scrap); envelope templates (JudiKins); embroidery floss; buttons; walnut ink

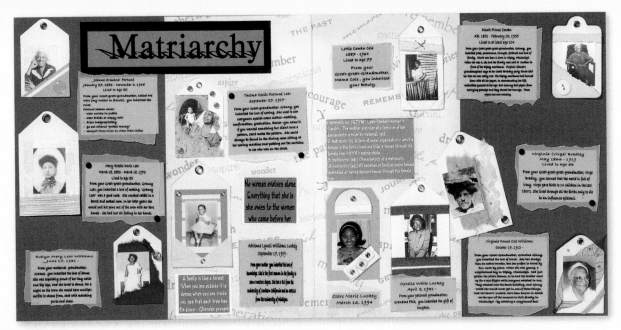

Matriarchy

EMBRACE ANCESTRAL GIFTS

Adrienne showcases ten women in her family whose gifts of strength and strong character have coalesced into the personality of her daughter. Embellish premade tags with layered papers, ribbon, fibers, eyelets, page pebbles, buttons, skeleton leaves and pre-made embellishments. Print title, genealogy information, matriarch defini-tion, photo captions and quotes on vellum and white and gold papers. Tear vellum edges; mount over tan cardstock. Attach with scrapbook nails.

Adrienne Luckey, Southfield, Michigan

patterned papers (Design Originals); premade tags and embellishments (Westrim); snaps (Chatterbox); wire; embroidery thread and page pebbles (Making Memories); ribbon; nails; brads; skeleton leaves; buttons

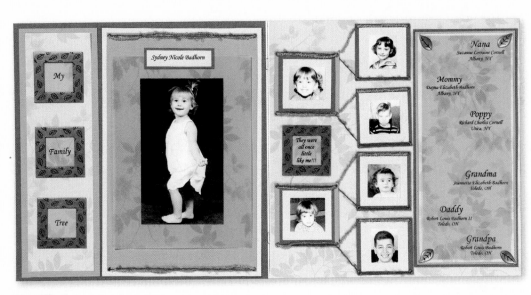

My Family Tree

REVEAL FAMILY RESEMBLANCE

Dayna's charming pedigree chart assembled with three generations of childhood photos provides a visual account of her daughter's family resemblance. Triple mat large photo on patterned vellum and solid cardstock; mount on rust cardstock background. Attach eyelets at corners of second mat; string fibers. Mat printed photo caption. Print title and family names on patterned vellum. Layer metal frames with vellum title words on double-matted patterned paper strip. Triple mat family names on solid and patterned papers; mount metal leaf eyelets at corners. Double and triple mat small photos; attach eyelets. String fibers through eyelets to show lineage.

Dayna Badhorn, Chandler, Arizona; Photos: Invu Portraits, Phoenix, Arizona

patterned vellum, papers, and fibers (EK Success); metal frames, eyelets, and leaf eyelets (Making Memories)

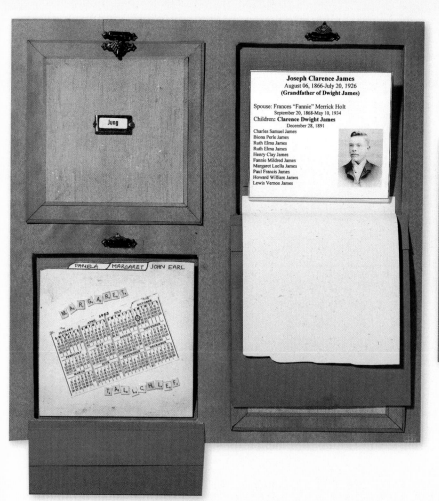

James Family History

FILE FAMILY HISTORY IN CABINET DRAWERS

Pam happily shares credit for the creation of her dimensional "filing cabinet" with her husband because of the hours he spent researching their family history as well as designing the folders filed inside the cabinet "drawers." Create dimensional drawers by cutting four same-sized windows in foam core using a ruler and craft knife. Cover front of foam core with wood-grain patterned paper. Create lined windows by slicing a large "x" inside each window on the back side of patterned paper mounted on foam core. Pull each of the four triangles in each window up and away from center of window. Adhere at back of foam core; cut off overhanging paper. Adhere brown cardstock background to back of foam core with spray adhesive. Print ancestral information and photos on white paper; accordion fold printed information. Use pattern on page 109 or freehand cut "file folder" from ivory cardstock; horizontally score and fold ½" from bottom of folder. Chalk and embellish with reduced color-copied family documents. Write surnames and details with black pen. Mount folder flap and printed information inside lined window as shown. Cut brown cardstock squares larger than windows for drawer fronts; horizontally score and fold ½" from bottom. Adhere folded flap just under lined window; flip up drawer front. Layer with brown patterned papers as shown; draw mitered corners with black pen. Adhere bookplate stickers over printed family names. Color silver decorative clasps with aging medium before mounting as drawer closures.

Pam and Thom James, Ventura, California

pattern on page 109; patterned papers (Creative Imaginations); bookplate stickers (EK Success); foam core; aging medium; brads; hinges

The Legacy

TRACE THE LEGACY OF A NAME

Melanie journals about the pride, importance and meaning behind her son's first and middle names. Print title, journaling and photo captions on brown cardstock; double mat title and journaling. Triple mat photos; mount photo caption on second mat.

Melanie Butt, Cartersville, Georgia

brown and navy cardstocks; patterned paper (Frances Meyer)

The Story of Us

RE-CREATE THE LOOK OF YESTERYEAR

Carolyn chronicles the story of her parents' immigration to Canada with classic colors and vintage embellishments. Trim matted photos with decorative scissors. Mount printed journaling and photos on patterned paper background with black photo corners. Adhere phrase and letter stickers. Embellish page with eyelets and premade vintage embellishments.

Carolyn Deline, Amherstburg, Ontario, Canada

patterned paper (Creative Imaginations); letter and phrase stickers (EK Success); premade embellishments (Ivy Cottage); corner punch (Marvy); photo corners; eyelets

Mothers and Daughters

PRESERVE MATRIARCHAL VALUES

Simple, elegant and ladylike embellishments adorn fold-out panels that contain descriptive biographical information about six generations of women in Nancy's family. Print ancestral information, biographical details and title on gray cardstock; tear title into strip. Layer torn pink, burgundy and gray cardstocks on black cardstock background; mount buttons. Mount matted photo, ancestral information and button on front of fold-out panel; mount biographical information inside.

Nancy Korf, Portland, Oregon

black, burgundy and pink cardstocks, buttons; charms; image-editing software (JASC Paint Shop)

The "Mystree" Behind the Face

PLANT AN ANCESTRAL GARDEN

Lori swirls dimensional garden-themed embellishments around sheer vellum pockets which contain layered photo tags. Attach torn vellum strips to patterned paper background with eyelets; string fibers through eyelets. Print names on clear labels and biographical information on white cardstock. Mount photos on brown tags; adhere name labels. Mount biographical information on burgundy tags. Layer tags together; attach with gold brad. Handcut title word; mount on matted black cardstock. Print balance of title words on colored cardstock; double mat. Embellish page with silk ivy leaves, flowers, dragonfly and butterfly.

Lori Hoffman, Shippensburg, Pennsylvania

patterned papers (Hot Off The Press); tags (American Tag); clear labels (Avery); flower buttons (Jesse James); brads; eyelets; fibers; silk vine; butterfly; dragonfly

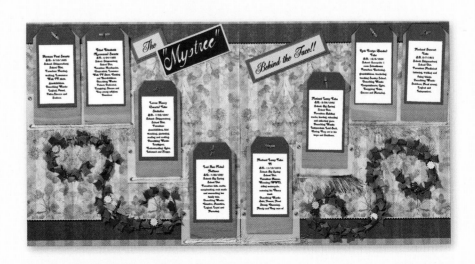

In My Family Tree

FOLLOW A FAMILY TRAIT

Sharon takes a tongue-in-cheek approach to the saying "the eyes have it" with photos that show generations of women in her family who all have the same facial features. Layer torn patterned paper, sliced cardstock strips, cork and mica tiles on black background cardstock. Single, double and triple mat photos; mount large snaps at top of three photos. Print photo captions, genealogy information and journaling on tan paper. Tear edges of journaling. Assemble title with metal letter tiles and word and letter stickers on torn cardstock. Embellish with themed stickers and mica tile. Slice twig stickers from large border sticker; adhere to look as if "piercing" title and journaling blocks.

Sharon Whitehead, Vernon, British Columbia, Canada; 2004 Memory Makers Master

patterned papers and themed stickers (Karen Foster Design); letter stickers (Colorbök); metal letters (Making Memories); mica tiles (USArtQuest); photo hangers (Tailorform); cork paper (Magic Scraps)

My Family Tree

COLLAGE DESCRIPTIVE WORDS

An assemblage of meaningful and descriptive words pays homage to Tammy's childhood memories of her beloved grandparents. Randomly adhere pieces of gold tissue paper on cardstock with gel matte medium; brush with acrylic paints and let dry. Stamp clock on background with black ink. Stamp dates and photo captions on ivory and brown cardstocks. Print ephemera clip art images, words and journaling on ivory cardstock; shade with chalk. Crop journaling into tag shape; tear edge. Punch hole and tie with brown fiber. Distress, crop and embellish clip art, dates and photo captions as shown. Tear photo edges; mat on brown cardstock with torn edges. Stamp butterfly and angel wings on ivory cardstock; color with chalks. Collage images, mesh, definition sticker, locket, gold elastic string, words and captions with matted photos. Emboss copper tags with metal letter stamps; embellish with curled wire.

Tammy Murdock, Victoria, British Columbia, Canada

matte medium gel (Golden); clock stamp (Inkadinkado); butterfly stamp (Magenta); tag template (Scrap Pagerz); letter stamps (Hero Arts); fibers (Rubba Dub Dub); date stamp, eyelets, and definition sticker (Making Memories); locket (Secret Village); metal letter stamps (House of Tools); copper (AMACO); mesh (Jest Charming); acrylic paint; tissue paper, chalk

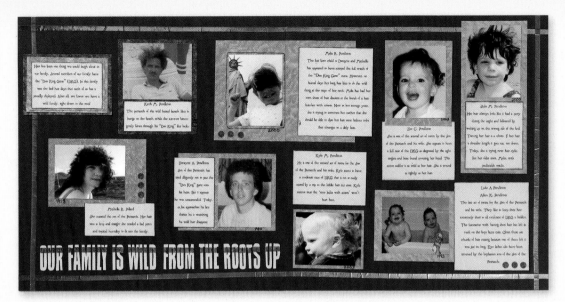

Our Family Is Wild

ENHANCE WILD ROOTS WITH METALLIC SHINE

Michelle presents a lighthearted look at how her family's wild roots have topped off three generations of Irish heads. Adhere copper tape border on black cardstock background. Print journaling on gray cardstock; ink edges. Mat photos and journaling on metallic patterned paper. Embellish mats with punched circles. Handcut title from light blue cardstock; adhere copper tape across letters; trim with craft knife.

Michelle Pendleton, Colorado Springs, Colorado

patterned papers (Emagination Crafts); copper tape (Venture Tape); hole punch

Marriage: the Link that Binds

DISPLAY WEDDING PORTRAITS

Brandi recognizes the matrimonial bond as the primary link of a generational chain with five genera-tions of wedding portraits alongside reduced copies of wedding certificates. Mat photos on green cardstock with black photo corners. Print title and text on transparency. Adhere stickers on patterned paper before layering under transparency; attach eyelets. Mount reduced copies of marriage certificates.

Brandi Ginn, Lafayette, Colorado; 2003 Memory Makers Master

patterned paper and stickers (Karen Foster Design); eyelets (Making Memories); photo corners (Canson)

Family

MOUNT CHART ON EMBELLISHED TAGS

A sepia-toned snapshot border and tagged pedigree chart provides an elegant overview of Joanna's ancestral history. Print family names in reverse on white cardstock; slice into strip. Layer with patterned papers on black cardstock background. Mount brown cardstock corners. Print genealogy chart on vellum; cut into sections and mat on tan cardstock. Layer on large tags cut from brown cardstock; attach eyelets. Punch hole at top of tag and tie with fibers. Scan and tint photos with image-editing software; mat on brown cardstock and arrange along bottom of page. Print title on cotton material; layer under metal bookplate and embellish with gold clock face.

Joanna Bolick, Fletcher, North Carolina; 2004 Memory Makers Master

patterned papers (K & Company); clock face (7 Gypsies); bookplate (Magic Scraps); eyelets; fibers; cotton materials

Some Family Trees...

OUTLINE LEAVES WITH CRAFT GLUE

Dana features some of the more colorful characters and fascinating stories she discovered in her family's history. Scan background photo; enlarge, lighten and add title with image-editing software. Print and double mat on peach and rust cardstocks. Freehand cut tree branch from rust cardstock. Layer with die-cut maple leaves outlined with white craft glue; let dry. Color dried glue with metallic rub-ons. Print ancestral stories on ivory cardstock; tear edges. Layer with torn green cardstock over tags cut from rust cardstock. Attach small brads on tags; secure fibers around brads before dangling from tree branches. Tie acorn charm with gold thread; dangle from small brad.

Dana Swords, Fredericksburg, Virginia

metallic rub-ons (Craf-T); acorn charm (All The Extras); fibers; mini brads; craft glue

Our "Hair"itage

SHOWCASE DISTINCTIVE HAIRSTYLES

Sharon and Dianna pay tribute to the fashionable, unique and sometimes humorous hairstyles worn by the women in their family. Layer solid and patterned papers on red cardstock background. Vertically wrap sheer ribbon around border on left page; tie bow. Stitch around blue patterned paper on right page. Attach small brads on both pages. Single and double mat photos, add corners or layer with black and torn red embossed cardstocks. Print photo captions and journaling on white cardstock; mat on black cardstock and layer with photos. Stamp title on white cardstock; double mat title and journaling on red embossed, black and patterned cardstocks. Attach flower made from graduating circles of torn patterned paper with small brad. Embellish pages with decorative bobby pins, scissors and heart.

Sharon Thiesen, Bourbonnais, Illinois; Dianna Dominguez, Pearland, Texas

patterned papers and letter stamps (Stampin' Up!); burgundy textured paper (K & Company); cream mulberry paper (Pulsar); brads (Making Memories); charms (Boutique Trims)

Roots

WALK THROUGH THE GARDEN OF LIFE

Jackie plants four generations of ancestral flowers in her family garden. Layer grass and garden path with gray and green cardstocks at bottom of blue cardstock background. Attach metal letter charms to premade picket fence with small eye pins. Shape cobblestones and title letters from colored clay and premade molds. Create a variety of flowers from textured and dimensional elements. Quill flowers with colored paper strips; mount twirled shapes around cropped photos. Cover die-cut flowers with tiny glass marbles, puff paint and seed beads; mount over photos when dry. Loop flower petals with tri-colored fibers; mount circle-cut photo at center and frame with tiny beads. Mount paper yarn flower stems as shown. Print genealogy information on vellum; layer over green or yellow patterned cardstocks and cut into leaf shapes. Stitch leaves to page with a French knot using green embroidery thread.

Jackie Gibson, Stafford, Texas

patterned paper (Leaving Prints); metal letter charms and fibers (Making Memories); quilling strips (Quilled Creations); puff paint (Jones Tones); beads (Westrim); wooden fence (Wood Shoppe); clay (Provo Craft); glass marbles; eye pins

My Family Is Bound by Love

ENCLOSE FAMILY'S LOVE BEHIND FOLD-OUT PANELS

Megan embraces family members with loving sentiments behind interlocking fold-out panels. Begin by making cover panels from vertically sliced pink cardstock; print phrases, sentiments and family names. Die cut heart in each panel; shade with chalk. Stamp mulberry paper with tree branches and flowers; mount behind heart window. Silhouette cut flowers from patterned cardstock; detail with crystal lacquer and mount with foam spacers. Embellish inside panels with punched and chalked squares, dimensional letters, crystal lacquer, glitter and wire swirls. Mat printed journaling; stamp flowers and adhere twig stickers. Assemble unique family tree chart with photo tags wrapped in vellum bands. Print sentiment for each family member on white cardstock. Cut tags from pink cardstock using template; mount photos and printed sentiment on each side of tag. Punch hole and tie with fibers. Print family names on green vellum; cut into strips. Form into band by folding strip around tag; adhere ends together. Assemble twig stickers into descendant chart lines; mount vellum bands along lines as shown. Slip tag through band; embellish with leaves punched from green solid and patterned papers and vellums. Lay panels over family tree page; hold together, punch circles on outer edges at 2" increments and bind with tied paper yarn. Center printed and matted title words vertically over both panels. Mount on alternating sides of panels creating an interlocking opening.

Megan Brent, Broomfield, Colorado

patterned papers (Bo-Bunny Press, Daisy D's); patterned vellum (Paper Garden); heart die cut (Accu-Cut); chalk; crystal lacquer (Sakura Hobby Craft); flower stamp (Stampin' Up!); tree branch stamp (Plaid); tag template (Create-a-Cut); twig stickers (Mrs. Grossman's); leaf punches (Paper Adventures); dimensional letter stickers (K & Company); paper yarn (Making Memories); wire; glitter; thread; 1½" square punch

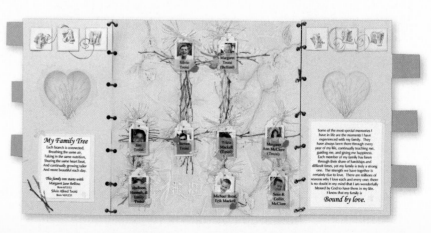

Hat Department

HANG A CURIOUS COLLECTION OF HATS

Heidi fashions an old-fashioned department store hat display next to showcases of ancestral photos of relatives wearing a variety of stylish headwear. Freehand draw and color hats, hat boxes and hatrack with colored pencils. Print price tag information on brown cardstock; cut into tag shape and mat. Punch small hole and tie with string. Assemble on hat rack; mount with foam spacers over patterned background paper as shown. Print title on tan cardstock; shade with colored chalks. Attach eyelets and tie with hemp string; "hang" over top of page. Slice three sides of same-sized squares in brown cardstock strip; score uncut side and fold back to create cabinet door. Shade with chalks; attach brads. Mount printed and chalked ancestral information inside cabinet doors and photos behind openings.

Heidi Schueller, Waukesha, Wisconsin; 2003 Memory Makers Master

patterned papers (Current); chalk; brads; eyelets; transparency; twine; hemp string

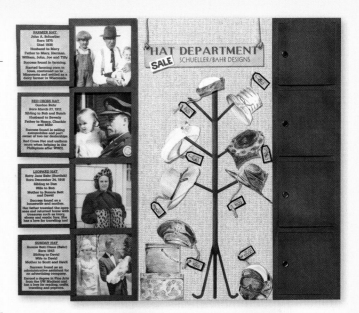

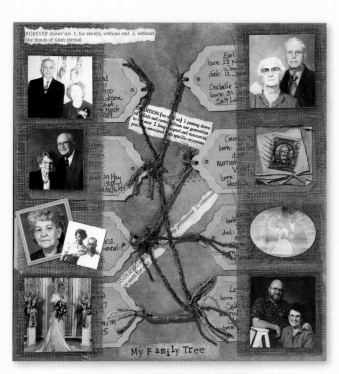

My Family Tree

TIE THE PRESENT TO THE PAST

Symbolic descendant lines demonstrate the fact that generations of Kym's family have stayed "tied" together since her ancestors came over on the Mayflower. Layer brown and ivory mesh border strips over patterned paper; adhere at horizontal 2¼" increments with two-sided tape to create pockets for informational tags. Mount photos and vintage sticker on mesh borders. Adhere title and definition stickers. Cut two sizes of tags from brown cardstocks using template. Layer tags, punch hole and tie with fibers. Write genealogy information on tags; secure in mesh pocket behind corresponding photo. Tie fibers together to demonstrate descendant lines.

Kym Smith, West Bountiful, Utah

patterned papers and themed stickers (Karen Foster Design); definition sticker (Making Memories); mesh (Magenta); tag template (Deluxe Designs); fibers

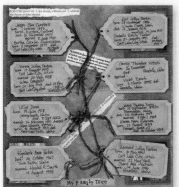

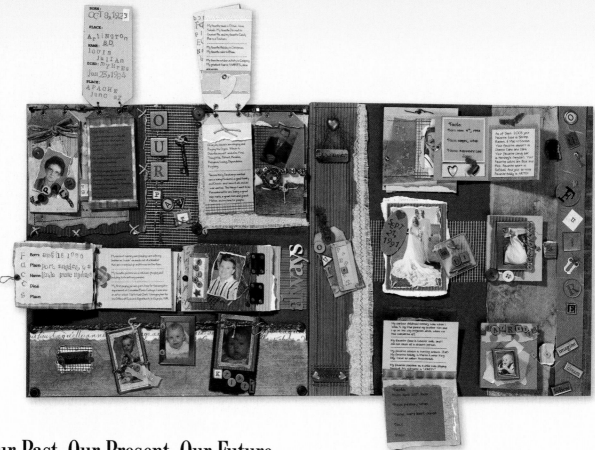

Our Past, Our Present, Our Future

CREATE A LIBRARY OF "STORY" BOOKLETS

After conducting family-member interviews, Trisha documents each person's "story" inside uniquely designed booklets. Create booklets from patterned and textured cardstocks; distress, stitch, stamp, embellish, ink and chalk covers. Print family "stories" on cardstock and patterned paper pages; score, fold and embellish with fibers, brads, buttons and torn vellum strips. Assemble booklet bindings from eyelets, brads, wires and hinges. Layer booklets over patterned vellum, mesh and cardstock strips on blue cardstock background. Assemble beginning of title on left page with metal letter tiles and conchos over mesh strip intertwined with fibers. Attach key with yarn. Rub word transfer onto vellum; stitch over patterned vellum strip. Mount metal word. Tear hole in green patterned paper strip; chalk and layer over mesh and metal word tag tied with twine.

Layer patterned papers at bottom of left page; attach metal snaps. Horizontally string fibers; mount, clip and hang matted and embellished baby photos. On right page, layer metal letters and frame with mesh on walnut ink-stained tag for second part of title; tie with fibers. Mount on torn corrugated cardstock and cheesecloth border; shade with chalk and machine stitch around edges. Dangle metal word tag from embossed heart with fibers. Mount metal word tag on mesh with heart brads. Complete title with a variety of metal and tag letters mounted on green cardstock strip; stitch letter tags with fibers. Mount word tags over mesh scrap.

Trisha Jones, Nephi, Utah

patterned and textured cardstocks (sources unknown); vellum; assorted fibers, brads, buttons, eyelets, brads, wires, hinges, mesh, tiles, conchos, mesh, key, clips, letter and word tags (sources unknown); ink; chalk; cheesecloth

Pendleton³ Family Circuit

CONNECT FAMILY INTERESTS

Dwayne's clever assembly of an electronically themed layout demonstrates the way in which three generations of men in his family stay connected. Punch small circles from a thin copper sheet; adhere with copper foil tape on green cardstock background to resemble electronic design. Draw black dots on punched circles. Mat photos on brown cardstock. Print title and journaling on vellum; attach electronic doodads. Mount circuit board.

Dwayne Pendleton, Colorado Springs, Colorado

copper foil tape (Venture Tape); copper sheet (AMACO); electronic doodads (Radio Shack); circle punch; circuit board

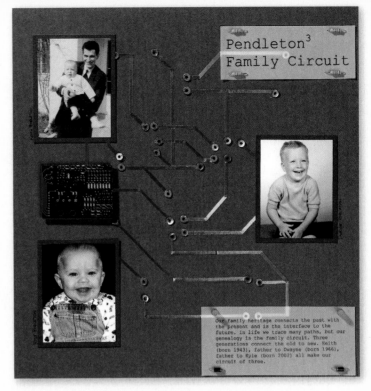

Our Family Tree

MAKE SLIDE MOUNT PHOTO FRAMES

Peggy's collection of photos includes the living "family tree" that has remained a symbol of strength and stability for over sixty years. Double mat photos with green and black cardstocks; mount on layered patterned paper background. Cut faux slide mounts from black cardstock; slice out window with craft knife and mount over photos. Embellish with tag stickers and eyelets; adhere word stickers on tags. Print title, definition, photo captions and journaling on tan cardstock; crumple, flatten, tear edges and chalk. Attach rivets to title blocks; string with fibers. Add metal letter tile on definition. Mat metal plaque on cardstock. Mount small photo on tag; attach to circle tag with eyelet.

Peggy Adair, Fort Smith, Arkansas

patterned papers (Daisy D's, Provo Craft, Rocky Mountain Scrapbook Company); tag stickers (EK Success); metal plaque (Making Memories); chalk; rivets; fiber; eyelets; tag

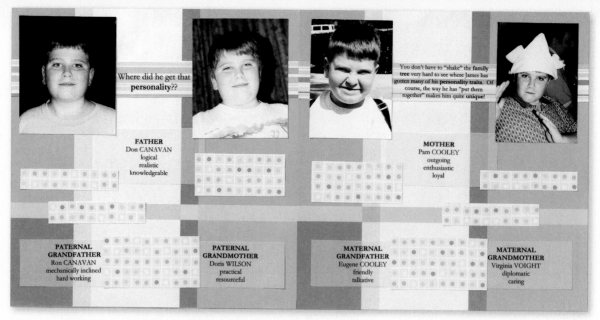

Where Did He Get That Personality?

RECOGNIZE FAMILIAR PERSONALITY TRAITS

Pam surrounds descriptions of ancestral personality traits that characterize her son's unique nature with quirky, geometric patterned papers. Print title, genealogy information and journaling on vellum; layer with patterned papers and photos on patterned paper background.

Pam Canavan, Clermont, Florida

patterned papers (KI Memories); vellum

Six Generations in Colorado

EMBOSS BACKGROUND DESIGN

Paula adds dimension and color to plain background paper with thematic embossed and inked designs. Single and double mat photos on colored cardstocks. Dry emboss tree design, outline of tree, pine cones and pine tree branches with brass stencils on white cardstock background. Color images with finger daubers and pigment ink. Crop tree design into circle; trim with decorative scissors and mat. Write title and photo captions with green pen and journaling with black fine-tip pen.

Paula Hallinan for Heritage Handcrafts, Littleton, Colorado

white and green cardstocks; brass stencils (Heritage Handcrafts); decorative scissors; embossing stylus; ink; green and black pens

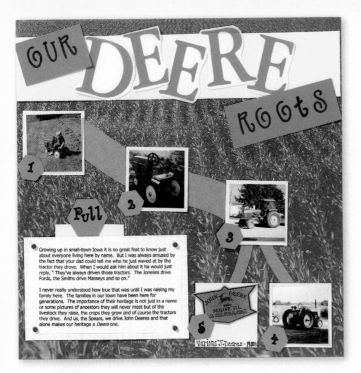

Our Deere Roots

DOCUMENT A GENERATIONAL FAVORITE

Michelle discovered how a piece of farming equipment could become a significant tie that binds three generations of her husband's family together. Write two title words on green cardstock using template; print green title word on white cardstock. Layer title words over yellow cardstock border mounted on patterned paper background. Mat photos and logo cut from patterned paper on yellow cardstock; layer along path cut from gray cardstock. Print family history on white cardstock; mat on yellow patterned paper and attach brads. Assemble pullout genealogy information from yellow cardstock and punched cardstock circle; slide behind journaling.

Michelle Spear, Milo, Iowa

patterned papers (Close To My Heart, Creative Imaginations, Wübie Prints); letter template (Pebbles); letter stickers (Making Memories); brads

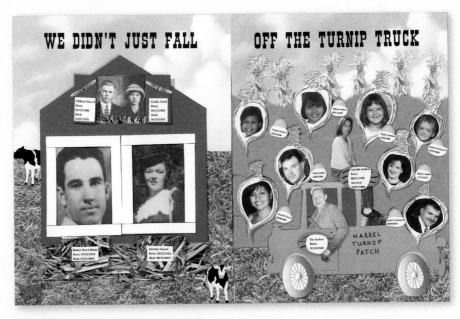

We Didn't Just Fall Off the Turnip Truck

ASSEMBLE A COLLAGED SCENE

Carolyn places ancestors and family members in a humorous collaged scene based on a favorite family saying. Print title on sky paper; layer with grass paper for background. Freehand draw and cut barn from red cardstock; slice, score and fold window. Mount over photo; attach brads from behind page. Frame large photos with white cardstock strips. Cut hay photo border with decorative scissors; adhere animal stickers. Print genealogy information on white cardstock. Freehand draw and cut turnip frames and watermelons; silhouette cut printed pumpkin and haystack clip art. Layer with photos and genealogy information on torn brown cardstock strips. Enhance truck clip art with silhouette-cut photos; write with black pen.

Carolyn Anders, Pittsburg, Texas

patterned papers (Frances Meyer); farm animal stickers (Crafts Etc., Mrs. Grossman's); hay photo border (Creative Imaginations); truck clip art (Hot Off The Press); computer clip art (Hallmark); decorative scissors; brads

My Family Tree

SPIRAL BIND MINI THEN AND NOW FLIPBOOKS

Beth stitches mini photo flipbooks to showcase then and now photos of her family and ancestors. Select photos, pairing a childhood photo with an adult photo of the same person. Scan the photos and enlarge or reduce until they are approximately the same size, print and crop into rounded rectangles. To make flip books, use avocado mulberry paper as base and decorate edges with embossing tape and gold embossing powder. Attach green suede with gold embroidery thread; mount childhood photo on the outside and adult photo on the inside along with personal information. Top booklets off with names and place page pebbles over names. Create gilded page borders and mount booklets in place. Use gold pen to write title down right edge of spread and saying at top of spread. Finish with felt leaf, paper and jute page accents.

Beth Cordes-Rackov, The Colony, Texas

mulberry papers; embossing tape; gold embossing powder and embossing heat gun; suede paper (Hot Off The Press); vellum; word stencil (American Traditional Designs); page pebbles (Making Memories); gold metallic embroidery thread and sewing needle; felt leaves (Colorbōk); gold metallic pen; wire; felt; embroidery floss; jute

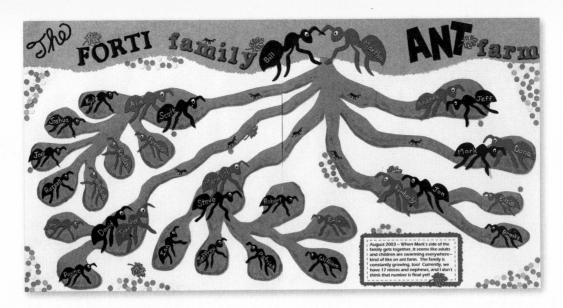

The Forti Family Ant Farm

EMBRACE UNUSUAL INSPIRATION

Dana proves that inspiration for unique layouts can come from the most unusual places. Her large and semi-chaotic atmosphere at family gatherings evoked memories of the ant farms Dana enjoyed observing as a child. Trim blue cardstock border with decorative scissors; mount along top of tan patterned cardstock background. Freehand cut underground ant tunnels to represent ancestral lines from brown cardstock; detail and shade with brown pencils and pens. Mount large and small die cut and sticker ants; add details and relative names with white and black gel pens. Print journaling on white cardstock; mat on red cardstock trimmed with decorative scissors. Adhere letter die cuts and shadowed stickers for title. Complete page with punched leaves and clusters of circles as shown.

Dana Forti, Claremont, California

patterned paper (Keeping Memories Alive); letter stickers (Creative Memories); ant stickers (Mrs. Grossman's); decorative scissors (Fiskars); letter die cuts; ant die cuts; leaf punch; hole punch

Strong Family Trees

MEMORIALIZE MILITARY SERVICE

Pam proudly pays tribute to her ancestors who dedicated years of their lives serving their country with military service. Layer heritage patterned papers for background. Print title and descriptive words, journaling and photo captions on vellum; tear around edges. Layer photo captions and descriptive words over patriotic-themed stickers; attach eyelets on printed vellum. Handcut title from patterned paper. Layer sticker embellishments over torn pieces of patterned paper and vellum.

Pam Canavan, Clermont, Florida

patterned papers and themed stickers (Karen Foster Design); eyelets; vellum

The Boston Tea Party

HONOR HISTORIC FREEDOM FIGHTERS

Jennifer floats handmade tea bags and memorabilia in a sea of symbolic remembrance for two relatives who helped make historic waves during the Revolutionary War. Tear two sides of tan cardstock; mount over patterned paper background. Layer torn cardstock in shades of blue along bottom of page. Print genealogy information on white cardstock; cut into large and small tags. Attach eyelet; tie with fibers to small tag. Mount circle-punched photo or silhouette on small tag. Fold vellum into "tea bag"; insert geneal-ogy tag and secure between torn cardstock layers. Punch circles from red and crumpled, flattened and chalked ivory cardstocks; adhere letter stickers for title and layer with foam spacers. Double mat picture and printed journaling on torn red and white cardstocks. Embellish journaling and photo mat with stitched button and brown satin ribbon. Hide journaling behind double-matted picture.

Jennifer Brunner, Dowagiac, Michigan

patterned papers (Daisy D's); letter stickers (Treehouse Designs); eyelets (Making Memories); tags (Avery, DMD); circle punch, brown ribbon; buttons

Little Family Tree

HONOR VETERANS WITH A PATRIOTIC MEMORIAL

Sue dedicates a patriotic memorial to her Netherlands ancestors who immigrated to America and served their new country in a number of historic wars. Mat patterned paper on burgundy cardstock for background. Freehand cut windmill body from patterned papers; mat and layer as shown. Layer roof "shingles" with rectangles punched from patterned paper. Print genealogy information on speckled cardstock; double mat on burgundy and blue cardstocks. Punch rectangle border at bottom of blue mat; mount over burgundy cardstock strips. Attach completed windmill blades at center of roof with gold brad as shown. Print title on patterned paper; tear top of strip and layer over blue paper at bottom of page. Embellish with stickers. Print photo captions, journaling and list on patterned paper. Mat photo, text and photo captions. Tear left edge of list; layer over torn blue paper. Embellish with stickers.

Sue Little, Poplar Bluff, Missouri

patterned papers (Creative Imaginations, Hot Off The Press, Karen Foster Design, Mustard Moon); stickers (Karen Foster Design); rectangle border punch; chalks

Family Treasure

DISCOVER BURIED TREASURE

Jane recognizes the real treasure in her ancestral history is the discovery of each relative's unique personality and achievements that makes them exceptional individuals. A collection of reduced copies of collaged layouts are made into fold-out elements that hide descriptive journaling. Tear and roll edges of tan cardstock; chalk to look like antique map before mounting on green cardstock background. Create fold-out panels by attaching cardstock strips behind reduced copy of scrapbook pages as shown. Fold strips in half and mount on page under printed journaling. Freehand draw and cut anchor and "x" from gold, burgundy and black cardstocks; wrap fibers around anchor. Mount "x" amongst matted coins and sliced paper strip trail. Handcut title and directional symbol from green cardstock. Mount shell nailheads next to sliced green cardstock grass.

Jane Swanson, Janesville, Wisconsin

black and tan cardstocks; fibers; coins (Boxer Scrapbook Productions); shell nailheads (All The Extras)

Patterns

Use these helpful patterns to complete scrapbook pages featured in this book. Enlarge a pattern by the percentage shown and photocopy the pattern. When transferring patterns to your paper of choice, be sure to cut on solid, continuous lines and fold dotted lines.

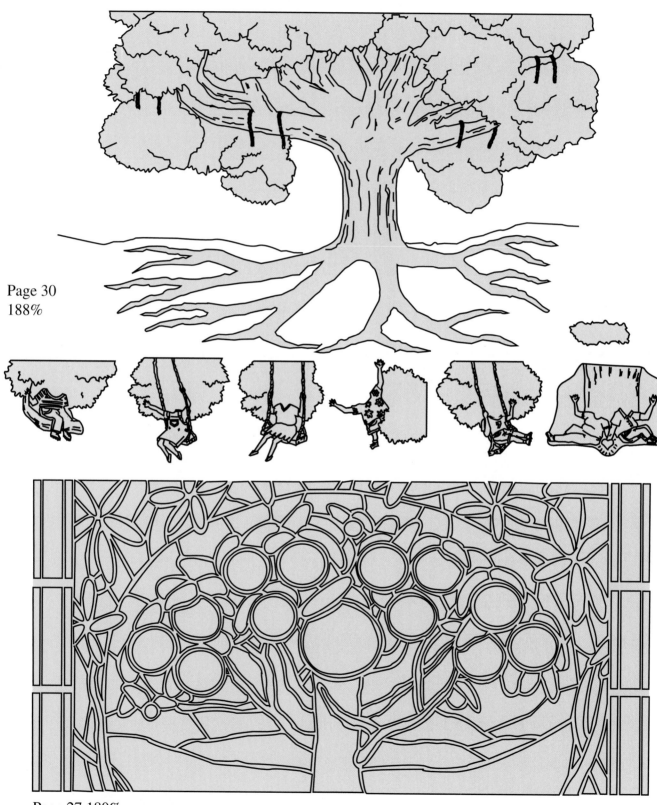

Page 30
188%

Page 27 180%

Page 38
170%

Page 69
100%

Page 26
160%

Page 68
160%

Rosemaling pattern © 2003 Joanne MacVey, Norsk Designs.

Page 90
150%

Page 84
150%

Additional Instructions & Credits

PAGE 1 FAMILY LEGACY

Layer torn patterned papers along bottom of purple cardstock background with inked edges; mount decorative corners. Form clay into tree trunk and branches; bake according to manufacturer's directions. Paint with acrylic paints; let dry before mounting silk leaves on tree with glue dots. Print genealogy information and numbers on green and lavender cardstocks. Ink edges of genealogy information before mounting on page. Print title on transparency; mount over torn border. Mat photos on lavender cardstock; ink edges. Mount square-punched printed numbers at upper right corner of photos and coordinating genealogy information.

Jodi Amidei, Memory Makers Books

patterned papers (Chatterbox, EK Success); transparency (Grafix); clay (Polyform Products); paints (Delta, Sanford); decorative metal corners (K & Company); silk leaves

PAGE 14 LUNENBURG LEGACY

Mix modeling paste with acrylic paint using a paint spatula; form tree trunk and branches on freezer paper and let dry. Shade with walnut ink. Peel tree from freezer paper; mount on patterned cardstock background. Cut journaling tags from green cardstock using template. Shade with chalk; attach tiny eyelets and tie with embroidery thread. Mount cropped photos and journaling squares on painted, sanded and stitched tin tiles. Secure silk leaves, tags and photo tiles on tree with glue dots. Create hinged journaling booklet from blue and green papers. Cut window frames from blue and green papers for fold-out title/journaling booklet; attach cardstock strips between layers as hinges. Mount layered frames over vellum. Handcut title letters; shade with chalk. Secure hinges under blue cardstock

mounted on page. Pierce holes; feed elastic string through holes and attach on back of page. Secure journaling under elastic string.

Lisa Dixon, East Brunswick, New Jersey

patterned paper (Club Scrap); modeling paste (Liquitex); acrylic paint (Delta); walnut ink and elastic string (7 Gypsies); silk leaves; stitched tin tiles (Making Memories); template (Deluxe Designs); embroidery floss; eyelets; chalks; freezer paper; brads

PAGE 40 BLUEPRINTS

Use genealogy or scrapbook software as Kristin did to create a fan chart. Draw and divide concentric circles using drawing tools, fill in family history information and print on vellum. Mount circle-cropped photos down left border; add word eyelets. Mount additional photos on tags and secure on color-blocked background with snaps. Finish with photo captions on vellum.

Kristin Contino, Milwaukee, Wisconsin; Photos: Robert Oelke, Schofield, Wisconsin

patterned papers (SEI); vellum; scrapbook software (Scrapbook Factory by Nova Development); word eyelets (Making Memories); white snaps

PAGE 60 SAINTS & SINNERS

Photos: Adam Richetti; Mother Pauline; Livingston Studios, New York; Akalites Studio, Mount Carmel, Pennsylvania; Black and White Studios, Arlington, Virginia

PAGE 64 A PIECE OF MY FAMILY TREE

Crop photos into ovals; mount on page. Photocopy and reduce document onto vellum. Create side border with layers of mulberry papers; attach eyelets, string fiber and mount on page. Print title, journaling and photo captions onto vellum; mat with mulberry paper and adhere. Mount photo captions with

chalk-colored vellum tags; tie with fibers and mount on page.

Cynthia McConnell-McNeil, Folkston, Georgia

patterned paper (K & Company); vellum; mulberry paper; chalk; eyelets; fibers

PAGE 68 AND 109 HAUGEN-HELLE TIES

Rosemaling pattern and painting by Joanne MacVey of Norsk Designs, 15 Aspen Drive, Blue Grass, Iowa 52726. (563) 381-2286 www.joannemacvey.com

PAGE 78 THE WALKER FAMILY

Mount torn cardstock along upper and lower borders across spread. Mount vellum and cardstock border on left edge of spread. Print title and saying on paper; wet, crumple, flatten and dry before adhering. Assemble gear collage with cheesecloth, stickers, fly and string; mount. Print story on vellum; adhere. Punch holes across upper and lower edges; thread cording in Xs through holes. Assemble accordion-style foldout with cardstock and patterned paper; cut frame in cover and emboss. Add photos and captions printed on vellum to fold-out; mount on page. Crop and mat smaller photos. Stamp fish, crop and mat; add captions, eyelets and swivels and mount over cheesecloth. Finish with final caption attached to fishing pole with wire.

Samantha Walker, Battle Ground, Washington

patterned paper (Flax Art & Design); fishing gear stickers (EK Success); embossing template (Fiskars); fish stamp (source unknown); cheesecloth; string; fishing swivels and fly; vellum; mini eyelets; oval, square and 1/16" circle punches; thin wooden dowel or stick; wire; faux leather cording

Sources

The following companies manufacture products featured in this book. Please check your local retailers to find these materials. In addition, we have made every attempt to properly credit the items mentioned in this book. We apologize to any company that we have listed incorrectly or the sources were unknown, and we would appreciate hearing from you.

3L Corp.
(800) 828-3130
www.scrapbook-adhesives.com

3M Stationery
(800) 364-3577
www.3m.com

7 Gypsies
(800) 588-6707
www.7gypsies.com

Accu-Cut® (wholesale only)
(800) 288-1670
www.accucut.com

Adobe
www.adobe.com

All My Memories
(888) 553-1998
www.allmymemories.com

All Night Media (see Plaid Enterprises)

All The Extras—no longer in business

American Art Clay Company (AMACO)
(800) 374-1600
www.amaco.com

American Crafts
(801) 226-0747
www.americancrafts.com

American Tag Company
(800) 223-3956
www.americantag.net

American Traditional Designs®
(800) 448-6656
www.americantraditional.com

Amscan, Inc.
(800) 444-8887
www.amscan.com

Anna Griffin, Inc (wholesale only)
(888) 817-8170
www.annagriffin.com

Autumn Leaves
(800) 588-6707
www.autumnleaves.com

Avery Dennison Corporation
(800) GO-AVERY
www.avery.com

Bazzill Basics Paper
(480) 558-8557
www.bazzillbasics.com

Beadery®, The
(401) 539-2432
www.thebeadery.com

Bo-Bunny Press
(801) 771-0481
www.bobunny.com

Boutique Trims, Inc.
(248) 437-2017
www.boutiquetrims.com

Boxer Scrapbook Productions
(503) 625-0455
www.boxerscrapbooks.com

Bright Eyes—no info available

Broderbund Software Corp.
(319) 247-3325
www.broderbund.com

Canson, Inc.®
(800) 628-9283
www.canson-us.com

Card Connection, The
—see Michaels

Carolee's Creations®
(435) 563-1100
www.carolees.com

Charm and Bead Collectibles
www.charmandbeadcollectibles.com

Chatterbox, Inc.
(208) 939-9133
www.chatterboxinc.com

Clearsnap, Inc.
(800) 448-4862
www.clearsnap.com

C-Line Products, Inc.
(800) 323-6084
www.C-lineproducts.com

Close To My Heart®
(888) 655-6552
www.closetomyheart.com

Club Scrap™
(888) 634-9100
www.clubscrap.com

Colorbök™, Inc. (wholesale only)
(800) 366-4660
www.colorbok.com

Craf-T Products
(507) 235-3996
www.craf-tproducts.com

Crafts, Etc., Ltd.
(800) 888-0321
www.craftsetc.com

Cranston Print Works
www.cranstonvillage.com

Create-a-Cut—no info available

Creative Imaginations
(wholesale only)
(800) 942-6487
www.cigift.com

Creative Impressions
(719) 596-4860
www.creativeimpressions.com

Creative Memories®
(800) 468-9335
www.creativememories.com

C-Thru® Ruler Company, The
(wholesale only)
(800) 243-8419
www.cthruruler.com

Current®, Inc.
(800) 848-2848
www.currentinc.com

Daisy D's Paper Company
(888) 601-8955
www.daisydspaper.com

Darice, Inc.
(800) 321-1494
www.darice.com

Delta Technical Coatings, Inc.
(800) 423-4135
www.deltacrafts.com

Deluxe Designs
(480) 497-9005
www.deluxecuts.com

Design Originals
(800) 877-7820
www.d-originals.com

DMC Corp.
(973) 589-0606
www.dmc.com

DMD Industries, Inc.
(wholesale only)
(800) 805-9890
www.dmdind.com

Dr. Ph. Martin's
(800) 843-8293
www.docmartins.com

EK Success™, Ltd.
(wholesale only)
(800) 524-1349
www.eksuccess.com

Elegant Scrapbooks—
no info available

Emagination Crafts, Inc.
(wholesale only)
(630) 833-9521
www.emaginationcrafts.com

Family Treasures, Inc.®
www.familytreasures.com

Family Tree Maker
(800) 548-1806
www.geneology.com

Fiskars, Inc. (wholesale only)
(715) 842-2091
www.fiskars.com

FLAX art & design
(415) 552-2355
www.flaxart.com

FoofaLa
(402) 330-3208
www.foofala.com

Frances Meyer, Inc.®
(800) 372-6237
www.francesmeyer.com

GBC Docubind—no info available

Generations—no info available

Global Solutions
(206) 343-5210
www.globalsolutionsonline.com

Golden Artist Colors, Inc.
(800) 959-6543
www.goldenacrylics.com

Grafix®/Graphic Art Systems, Inc.
(800) 447-2349
www.grafixarts.com

Graphic Products Corporation
(800) 323-1660
www.gpcpapers.com

Great Impressions Rubber
Stamps, Inc.
(800) 373-5908
www.greatimpressionsstamps.com

Halcraft USA
(212) 376-1580
www.halcraft.com

Hallmark
www.hallmark.com

Heritage Handcrafts
(303) 683-0963

Heritage Hearts
(801) 427-3928

Hero Arts® Rubber Stamps, Inc.
(wholesale only)
(800) 822-4376
www.heroarts.com

Hot Off The Press, Inc.
(800) 227-9595
www.paperpizazz.com

House of Tools—no info available

Impress Rubber Stamps
(206) 901-9101
www.impressrubberstamps.com

Inkadinkado® Rubber Stamps
(800) 888-4652
www.inkadinkado.com

Ivy Cottage Creations
(888) 303-1375
www.ivycottagecreations.com

Jacquard Products/Rupert, Gibbon
& Spider, Inc.
(800) 442-0455
www.jacquardproducts.com

Jasc Software
(800) 622-2793
www.jasc.com

Jesse James & Co., Inc.
(610) 435-0201
www.jessejamesbutton.com

Jest Charming
(702) 564-5101
www.jestcharming.com

Jones Tones
(719) 948-0048
www.jonestones.com

JudiKins
(310) 515-1115
www.judikins.com

K & Company
(888) 244-2083
www.kandcompany.com

Karen Foster Design™
(wholesale only)
(801) 451-9779
www.karenfosterdesign.com

Keeping Memories Alive
(800) 419-4949
www.scrapbooks.com

KI Memories
(469) 633-9665
www.kimemories.com

Krylon
(216) 566-2000
www.krylon.com

Leaving Prints™
(801) 426-0636
www.leavingprints.com

Leister Productions
(717) 697-1378
www.LeisterPro.com

Li'l Davis Designs
(949) 838-0344
www.lildavisdesigns.com

Liquitex® Artist Materials
(888) 4-ACRYLIC
www.liquitex.com

Magenta Rubber Stamps
(wholesale only)
(800) 565-5254
www.magentarubberstamps.com

Magic Mesh™
(651) 345-6374
www.magicmesh.com

Magic Scraps™
(972) 238-1838
www.magicscraps.com

Making Memories
(800) 286-5263
www.makingmemories.com

Mamelok Press
www.mamelok.com

Marcus Brothers Textiles, Inc.
(212) 354-8700
www.marcusbrothers.com

Martha Stewart
www.marthastewart.com

Marvy® Uchida (wholesale only)
(800) 541-5877
www.uchida.com

Ma Vinci's Reliquary
www.crafts.dm.net

McGill, Inc.
(800) 982-9884
www.mcgillinc.com

McGonigal Paper and Graphics
www.mcgpaper.com

me & my BiG ideas®
(wholesale only)
(949) 583-2065
www.meandmybigideas.com

Michaels® Arts & Crafts
(800) MICHAELS
www.michaels.com

Microsoft Corporation
www.microsoft.com

Mrs. Grossman's Paper Co.
(wholesale only)
(800) 429-4549
www.mrsgrossmans.com

Mustard Moon™
(408) 229-8542
www.mustardmoon.com

My Mind's Eye™, Inc.
(801) 298-3709
www.frame-ups.com

Nature's Handmade Paper, LLC
(800) 861-7050
www.natureshandmadepaper.com

Nova Development Corporation
(818) 591-9600
www.novadevelopment.com

NRN Designs
(800) 421-6958
www.nrndesigns.com

Nunn Design
(360) 379-3557
www.nunndesign.com

Offray
www.offray.com

Once Upon A Scribble™
(702) 896-2181
www.onceuponascribble.com

Paper Adventures®
(wholesale only)
(800) 727-0699
www.paperadventures.com

Paper Garden, Inc.
(435) 867-6398
www.mypapergarden.com

Paper Loft, The
(866) 254-1961
www.paperloft.com

Paper Patch®, The
(800) 397-2737
www.paperpatch.com

Paperbilities—no info available

Pebbles, Inc.
(800) 438-8153
www.pebblesinc.com

Penny Black Inc.
(510) 849-1883
www.pennyblackinc.com

Pixie Press
(888) 834-2883
www.pixiepress.com

Plaid Enterprises, Inc.
(800) 842-4197
www.plaidonline.com

Polaroid
www.polaroid.com

Polyform Products Co.
(847) 427-0020
www.sculpey.com

Provo Craft® (wholesale only)
(888) 577-3545
www.provocraft.com

PSX Design™
(800) 782-6748
www.psxdesign.com

Pulsar Paper Products
(877) 861-0031
www.pulsarpaper.com

Punch Bunch, The
(254) 791-4209
www.thepunchbunch.com

Purple Onion Designs
www.purpleoniondesigns.com

Quark, Inc.
(303) 894-8888
www.quark.com

QuicKutz™
(888) 702-1146
www.quickutz.com

Quilled Creations
(858) 388-0706
www.quilledcreations.com

Radio Shack
(800) THE SHACK
www.radioshack.com

Ranger Industries, Inc.
(800) 244-2211
www.rangerink.com

Rocky Mountain Scrapbook Co.
(801) 785-9695
www.rmscrapbook.com

Rollabind LLC
(800) 438-3542
www.rollabind.com

Rubba Dub Dub
(707) 748-0929
www.artsanctum.com

Rubber Stampede
(800) 423-4135
www.rubberstampede.com

Rusty Pickle
(801) 272-2280
www.rustypickle.com

Sakura Hobby Craft
(310) 212-7878
www.sakuracraft.com

Sandylion Sticker Designs
(800) 387-4215
www.sandylion.com

Sanford Corp.
(800) 323-0749
www.sanfordcorp.com

Scrapbook Sally
(509) 329-1591
www.scrapbooksally.com

Scrap Ease®
(800) 272-3874
www.whatsnewltd.com

ScrapGoods™
a division of The Scrap Pack
www.scrapgoods.com

Scrap Pagerz™
(435) 645-0696
www.scrappagerz.com

Scrapworks, LLC
(801) 363-1010
www.scrapworksllc.com

Secret Village—no info available

SEI, Inc.
(800) 333-3279
www.shopsei.com

Sizzix
(866) 742-4447
www.sizzix.com

Sonburn, Inc. (wholesale only)
(800) 527-7505
www.theroyalstore.com

Staedtler®, Inc.
(800) 927-7723
www.staedtler-usa.com

Stampa Rosa, Inc.
no longer in business

Stampendous!®
(800) 869-0474
www.stampendous.com

Stampin' Up!®
(800) 782-6787
www.stampinup.com

Stampland
www.stamplandchicago.com

Stamps by Judith
www.stampsbyjudith.com

Sticker Studio™
(208) 322-2465
www.stickerstudio.com

Strathmore Papers
(800) 628-8816
www.strathmoreartist.com

Tailorform—no info available

Treehouse Designs
(501) 372-1109
www.treehouse-designs.com

Tsukineko®, Inc.
(800) 769-6633
www.tsukineko.com

Tumblebeasts Stickers
(505) 323-5554
www.tumblebeasts.com

USArtQuest
(800) 200-7848
www.usartquest.com

Venture Tape
(800) 343-1076
www.venturetape.com

Westrim® Crafts
(800) 727-2727
www.westrimcrafts.com

Wish in the Wind, LLC
(757) 564-6400
www.wishinthewind.com

Wood Shoppe—no info available

WorldWin Paper
(608) 834-9900
www.thepapermill.com

Wübie Prints
(888) 256-0107
www.wubieprints.com

Index